T0381114

FAITH POEMS

I Found My

Voice:

A

Gift

From God

EILEEN M. PHELPS

WESTBOW
PRESS®
A DIVISION OF THOMAS NELSON
& ZONDERVAN

WestBow Press books may be ordered through booksellers or by contacting:

WestBow Press
A Division of Thomas Nelson & Zondervan
1663 Liberty Drive
Bloomington, IN 47403
www.westbowpress.com
844-714-3454

ISBN: 979-8-3850-0644-1 (sc)
ISBN: 979-8-3850-0645-8 (hc)
ISBN: 979-8-3850-0646-5 (e)

Library of Congress Control Number: 2023916399

Print information available on the last page.

WestBow Press rev. date: 10/17/2023

CONTENTS

CHARACTERISTICS

DEVELOPING

FEELING

HEALING

INQUIRING

JUSTICE

LEARNING

MOTIVATION

THEME

QUALITIES

INTRODUCTION

A few of my poems were written in the years prior to 2019. Many of these poems were written in the years of the pandemic. It was an outlet to handle some of the losses my family experienced through this time.

Many friends and family members encouraged me in my writing. My wonderful husband was the one who encouraged me the most. I would give him my poems to read and critique. I always knew I would get honest feedback.

I always said I would not seek publication until I felt God's nudge. I know God gave me the words. As I sat at my computer, sometimes in the early morning hours, I would type. Often, the words would form over several days. I tried to stop a few times, but God was not done providing the words.

I would like to thank Women for Christ, United Women in Faith, Wesley Fellowship United Methodist Church, and Highlands United Methodist Church for giving me a platform for my poetry. My poems have been in the monthly newsletter for Women for Christ for the last year. Kay Owens, who was the editor during that time, would request a poem that fit the month. When I taught Sunday School (as a substitute) at Highlands, I would read a poem that related to the lesson. Wesley Fellowship, my church, put some of my poems in the bulletin. I even read a few during the church service. I have participated in a number of United Women in Faith programs that used some of my poems. I hope to widen the reach of my poems by publishing.

I would also like to thank my DBSA (Depression Bipolar Support Alliance) group who have been my greatest supporters. Many of my poems deal with mental illness and my journey with Bipolar, now over 32 years. I have been a member of this support group since 2012.

I have several very good friends to thank also. Linda has been my friend for 44 years. She inspired "My Sister, My Friend." I have two other friends, Edith and Glenda, who I have shared most of my poems with. They both have a very deep faith that has helped them through some difficult times.

I am dedicating this book to the Phelps family who welcomed me into the family over 48 years ago. I really miss my brother-in-law, James, who I am sure is leading a choir up in Heaven. I am also missing my other mother, Margaret Lois, who always treated me as a daughter.

BEING

Luke 15:23-24 "Then bring the fattened calf and slaughter it, and let's celebrate with a feast, because this son of mine was dead and is alive again; he was lost and is found." So, they began to celebrate.

A NURSE

I have been a nurse for fifty years,
Present through many moments filled with tears.
What I most remember is helping to allay any fears
As the time approached and death neared.
I began my nursing journey at seventeen,
Not having experienced life much in between.
I started into nursing school,
Before I had officially graduated high school.
We started with a group numbering thirty-four.
In summer, a few were lost; fall brought many more.
Those who remained considered the cost,
Counted the life of a nurse worth more than what was lost.

WHO AM I?

I am a child of God,
Loved beyond measure,
Uplifted by His grace,
Totally undeserving.

My body is His temple.
Many gifts are given me,
To use in His honor
And to glorify the Lord.

I am His creation,
As is everything on Earth.
He made me special,
Allowing me free will.

I have the choice to follow,
Surrender all to Him,
Freely give up my will,
And do His will instead.

He gave us ten commandments.
But stresses only two:
To love the Lord God with all my soul, body, and mind,
And to love myself and others, putting others first.

His love is not determined,
By anything I do.
His love has no regard for my actions.
It matters not what I do.

He opens my eyes to see.
Opportunities given me daily.
People are placed on my journey,
To allow growth in my faith.

In times of trouble and turmoil,
He is always there for me.
He gives me strength and purpose,
To overcome any trials along the way.

He sent Jesus into the world,
To live and die for me.
His crucifixion on the cross
Fully paid for my sin.

The cross was the beginning,
Not the end, as it was seen.
Afterward came His resurrection.
Now Jesus lives in me.

SERVANT

Have you ever wondered about the word "servant"?
I believe there are two parts to this word.
Jesus demonstrated a servant's role, although He is Lord.
First, how humility and other characteristics are shown,
The way the heart of the servant has grown.
No longer putting self-first,
Often accepting people at their worst.
The other part is the action that person takes,
Doing for others the moment the servant awakes.
I hope that my life will be lived as a servant,
Showing others how to live and prevent.
A life where time and talents are wasted.
Our accomplishments are not pasted,
Or focused on lifting ourselves up and boasting.
Displaying the opposite role, a master,
Creating pride in self, turning our lives into disasters.

IN THE MORNING

In the morning, I am inspired.
As I arise, no longer tired,
I gather the thoughts in my mind.
Going forth, I seek to find,
A place to sit and write,
Trying not to sound too trite.
In the morning, I have a clarity.
That sometimes is a rarity.
My thoughts can congeal,
And often these thoughts reveal.
A side of me I may conceal.
In the morning, I am more open.
I can often write, putting to pen,
The many thoughts I have.
Often, my sanity to save.

REDEEMED

I am redeemed by God's love,
Recognizing His great power from above.
My selfishness is replaced by care of others,
Understanding why a Christian bothers
To reach out, so I can really see.
How to love, because God first loved me.
He sent His Son to redeem,
All humankind and invite us to dream,
Of peace on Earth, a new creation.
Born in every nation to a different station,
Kingdom heirs as children of God.
Redeemed by His grace through Jesus's body and blood.

LEGACY

I have had several years to reflect on my legacy.
What words of wisdom will I impart to my loved ones?
How will they remember me when I depart this world?
I believe they will remember the time I spent with them.
I told them often that I loved them.
Actions we take to show that love dwells in our memory.
Daily, take the time to speak and show your love.
We can't turn back time or have a do-over.
The legacy of love will last much longer,
And be the treasure you leave behind.

FAMILY

There are many kinds of families.
One important family is the family of God.
An oldie but goodie from early rock and roll,
"We are Family," talks about "brothers and sisters."
It is one of my favorite songs of the late sixties.
I grew up in Philadelphia, the city of brotherly love.
Although I had one brother and one sister,
I had a large extended family,
And friends who became family.
Sometimes, we lose that sense of family.
Family provides love, stability, and encouragement.
Loss of family would be difficult.
We need to remember how important family can be.

COURAGE

Some say courage is the absence of fear.
I say it is to act even when fear is near.
Having courage to be yourself, not hiding
Behind some better version, guarding,
Against what others may think of you.
Hiding behind a mask,
Hoping for someone to ask.
If whom you present outwardly is the real you,
Never providing a single clue
Or possessing the courage to be an authentic you.

QUIET

It is in the quiet that I can rest.
No noise to interrupt my thoughts, to test,
My patience as I take a break.
Allowing any plan to slowly formulate and leak,
Into my consciousness over time.
Letting the quiet penetrate my mind as a prime
Way to stay in the here and now.
Moving gradually from the present to show
How a quiet person can be a force,
A guiding light to a contented future on a course
Laid down by quiet perseverance,
Receiving God's wonderful assurance.

TRANSFORMED

I am a new creation.
Totally transformed,
Acknowledging the change made
And the small part I played,
In how God transformed me.
Chains of pride and selfishness lifted, I am free.
Not trying on my own to be who God wants me to be.
Showing others in my actions so they can see.
The wonderful transformation that God has worked in me.
Giving Him the glory for all the changes
And the opportunities He arranges,
To witness to others "a transformed me."

AUTHENTIC

I try very hard to be an authentic me,
To be the "real" person that other people see.
Too often, I get scared because I am not,
Who others want me to be, so I am caught,
In a web of deceit, not being authentic.
Racing at a pace so frantic
To unite the person others see
With the true, "authentic" me.
Needing to know myself completely,
Not the sum of parts arranged so neatly,
Pleasing to others but not to me.
I can identify those parts not meant to be.
It is only then that I can see,
A truly wonderful person and be an "authentic "me.
The one whom God created me to be.

VULNERABLE

To be vulnerable is to show courage,
Very hard to let myself be vulnerable at this age.
Allowing myself to trust is a must.
Opening myself up to live a full life.
Not shielding myself from what could be bad.
Letting every experience, I 've ever had
Be fully felt, not pushed down or locked away.
Hoping for a better day,
Not feeling I must hide.
I can choose to ride along the tide,
Being vulnerable each day,
Seeking God to show the way.

CLARITY

It is my hope that clarity will be a gift,
From God so I will not be set adrift.
Wandering in a fog with no clear view,
Whittling down so many thoughts to just a few.
Hoping that clarity will rule my day,
And I will continue to find my way.
That clarity of thought will I display,
As I am led my part to play
In any plan God has for me.
Clarity showing what is to be.

STATUS

When I was younger, status was important.
I viewed it as a portent,
Of whom I was to become.
All the steps needed to come,
Before I reached the top rung,
Feeling that my identity hung
On the status I desired.
Many times, my situation left me tired.
Not able to reach the status when I started.
But as all my time and energy darted
To reach this goal in life,
It was as if someone took a knife.
My status was slashed into shreds,
Knitting together many threads,
And I was allowed to see.
Status is not what is meant to be.
It is not what God desires for me.

LEADING

I always thought I was better at following.
Often, I was called to a position of leading.
I never felt very comfortable in this role.
In many instances, leading took its toll.
One day, I had an insight on how to lead.
In my mind, God planted a seed.
I was trying to lead in a way not my own.
I was anxious, leading others into the unknown.
I could lead with God in an effective way.
It gives me courage to this day.

IN GOD'S STRENGTH

It is in my weakness that God's strength is revealed.
When I am unsure of myself, my next steps concealed,
It is God's strength that sees me through,
Allowing me to recognize what is true.
I can venture forth with renewed vision.
His strength is my provision.
God's strength lets me soar,
Leaving me wanting so much more.
Time to spend in His strength,
Witnessing the very breadth
Of what His power and strength can do.
His strength will lift you up too.

SANCTUARY

Sanctuary is most often seen as a place,
But I think of sanctuary as God's grace.
I can be at rest and peace,
No tension or anything to crease.
The security of being in His arms,
Not needing any charms,
To enable me to relax.
Allowing nothing to tax,
My ability to recover in His shelter,
Viewing nothing out of kilter.
I seek God when I need sanctuary in my life.
He walks with me, helping me to overcome strife.

REFLECTION

As I grow older, I have more reflection in my mind.
It is in this reflection that I find I am often unkind.
I speak, saying the words before I think.
My friendships come to the brink.
Compromised before my eyes can blink.
Reflection can bring me down.
Facing life with a frown.
But, if I am positive, in my reflection,
I can use it as an instrument of detection.
Not seeking a life of perfection,
Reflection can't change the past.
It can help me accept myself at last.

SOLITUDE

I seek solitude on occasion to regroup.
It is hard to find a place where I can recoup.
It is during solitude that I discover.
Solitude may sound lonely, but I do recover.
Recognizing what is important in life to do.
To be alone to think things through,
Knowing God is with me in my solitude.
Giving me guidance and changing my attitude.
My best thoughts and plans spring forth.
In solitude, I find my true North.

BEAUTY

There is beauty in each day, if we look.
In distractions, our time and energy took,
Away from seeing the beauty before our eyes.
We fail to enjoy the natural beauty that lies,
Within our grasp, failing to clasp.
The beauty that quickly passes us by.
This lack of attention may be why.
Beauty that lasts is viewed as existing in the past.

WAITING

I have always found it difficult to wait.
Sometimes it came from my fear of being late.
Mostly, it was the absence of patience.
As I never developed the experience,
Needed to see the value of waiting.
I always seemed to be salivating,
For good things to come quickly to me
Not being able to foresee.
The wonderful gift of waiting as things develop.
Allowing the patience, I prayed for to envelop.
Transforming me into a person waiting.
All my fears abating.

UNSPOKEN

I have left words unspoken, often feeling broken,
Because of the lack of expression and the feeling tension.
I left important words unsaid.
Sometimes, having a feeling of dread,
Of how those words, when spoken
Would be viewed as a token.
Not fulfilling in any way to build a bridge,
To meet somewhere in the middle, no umbrage.
But leaving words unspoken never solves what is broken.
God, grant me the courage to say what is unspoken.

*LOST, NOW FOUND

There are many lost moments, days, years in my life.
Oh, that I could cut away those lost times with a knife.
But it took those lost times to be found.
Discovering, in myself, a new identity.
No longer striving in my own entity.
God found me, leading me in His strength.
Across an abyss so huge in width and length,
Never could I have reached the other side.
If God had not turned the tide,
Allowing His presence to preside

UPHEAVAL

A painful experience is upheaval, turning everything upside down.
It is akin to being in a small boat on a raging sea, about to drown.
Knowing that nothing I can do will help in this matter.
All my pride in my accomplishments will shatter.
Upheaval demonstrates that God is in control always.
Recognizing that prayer is one of the best ways,
To survive the resulting upsets that upheaval brings.
I have found prayer to be the answer to most things.
When my life is in upheaval, I pray.
It is the only way to save the day.

PRESENT IN THE PAST

Being present in the past, I find no joy that will last.
Every day is a repeat of the day before,
With no gain in what I learn, nothing more.
It was hard to live with one foot in the past.
Never letting go so I can cast,
Away the shadows of what went before.
It is in letting go of the weight I bore.
The past mistakes I cannot change.
The previous life I fail to rearrange.
Knowing that it is best to leave the past,
Where it belongs, opening myself to see the vast
Joyous opportunities of living in the present.
No longer seeming to resent the days spent.
Being present in the past.

PURSUIT OF DREAMS

Over the years, my pursuit of dreams has changed.
At the beginning, I had a rigid plan arranged,
To see my dream fulfilled by my plan.
Only to find that no dream is fulfilled by man.
The dreams of my youth are not my dreams today.
Some of my dreams were met in such a way.
I know it was a dream that was supposed to be.
Other dreams grew so I could see.
Bigger dreams were possible for me.
The pursuit of dreams should never stop.
Dreams can be so over the top,
As they come true, I can feel my mouth drop.

REDEEMED

It takes my breath away to realize.
I am redeemed as I feel my life crystalize,
Into a new way of thinking and being.
No longer dwelling on the past, just seeing,
A new purpose in my life as I go forward.
Chains of sin removed as I travel toward,
A freedom I have never felt before.
Allowing myself to turn away and ignore.
The past mistakes and crooked roads I took.
No longer do I have to look.
Forever, I can live in the crook,
Of God's arms as I fit into his plan for me.
I am redeemed for all to see.

REJOICE

In each moment, I choose to rejoice.
As I do so, I hear God's small, still voice.
Every trial I go through I can feel His presence.
As I rejoice in Him, I can sense,
His response and love for me.
I know I am not alone.
Meeting my trials, sometimes having to atone.
Because I fail to turn to Him.
Making any chance of success slim,
In overcoming my trial and rejoice.
Failing to make the right choice,
And not hearing God's small, still voice.

MY SOUL THIRSTS

In times of trouble, my soul thirsts
In daily obstacles, my soul thirsts
In viewing unkindness, my soul thirsts
It thirsts for the living water only God can provide.
When others judge unfairly, my soul thirsts.
When I am disregarded, my soul thirsts.
When I am put aside, my soul thirsts.
It thirsts for the living water only God can provide.
As I live in a broken world, my soul thirsts.
As I fail to keep a promise, my soul thirsts.
As I do not speak of injustice, my soul thirsts.
It thirsts for living water only God can provide.

BEING IN HARMONY

Blending our voices together to sing in harmony.
No one sings out with a different tune.
Building a melody with seamless accord
As alto, soprano, tenor and bass sing as one.

Harmony brings a pleasant sound.
As one voice builds around the other voices,
To add layers to a song
Enhancing the beauty of the tune

Harmony is not just present in music, though.
Harmony in life can be achieved,
If we build up, we will not break down.
Enhancing the beauty in our life.

Harmony may be misunderstood.
Seen as giving up our own identity to blend.
I view harmony as adding to the wonder,
Of blending voices to make a greater good.

BEING AN ADVOCATE

In growing older, my role as an advocate has grown.
I have adopted the character of an advocate as my own.
As a retired nurse, accompanying someone to a visit,
With a medical professional or procedure where I sit.

Sometimes, it is just my presence that is required.
It could be listening closely to what is said.
Because the person I accompany is too worried or tired,
To hear all the information that was relayed.

Many times, it is my advice they seek.
I will not go beyond my role but offer a peek.
At the options they have for the decision they make,
They have an informed path to take.

I may be an advocate for the family as a whole,
When I think there is pressure that will take a toll.
Acting too quickly while feeling unsure,
Whether the steps taken will provide a cure.

BEING HUMBLE

Being humble is a trait not pursued.
Choosing to be boastful, loud, and crude
Allows us to think being humble shows us to be weak.
It is not a title that many people seek.

Being humble goes against the character.
Present in our society today, it is a factor.
We think will get in the way of the display.
Being the kind of person who will lead the way.

Wanting to be first, leading others forward.
Looked up to and favored as we moved toward.
A goal where we are the best at what we do.
Getting recognized, honored, and praised too.

Being humble is seen as being walked over,
Left behind by others, not a shaker or a mover.
Unwilling to be seen as less than.
I think being humble is being the best man.

MY SISTER, MY FRIEND

Over the years, you have become,
My sister, not just a dear friend.
A bond forged many years ago, prepared.
So many memories to be shared.

Though years have passed
This friendship grew to last.
Separated by distance in miles,
When again we met, we were wreathed in smiles.

A love of creating was part of that bond.
Along with showing the things of which we were fond,
Able to share with each other,
Always freely enjoying one another.

BEING A PERSON
OF PEACE

Being a person of peace requires a choice,
In how you turn out noise and use your voice.
I think of Isaiah writing about being still.
Hearing a small voice revealing God's Will.

Anger and shouting only magnifies discord.
When a quiet, reasoned voice gives word,
And peace and harmony are restored.
Providing a plan to go forward.

Being a person of peace means listening,
To what is said and not said, hastening.
To make a safe place to share,
Hurt feelings to spare,

Being a person of peace, not always right
Choosing to see another's plight.
Working together to right a wrong.
Peacefully showing how to be strong.

CHARACTERISTICS

Psalm 4:4 "Be angry and do not sin; on your bed, reflect in your heart and be still."

TRUST

Trust allows you to share and be completely open.
Fear of rejection can lead you into a tailspin.
When we counter fear with faith, trust can develop.
Allowing an increasing openness to envelop,
As we learn to trust the one who brought us into being.
Knowing we can trust in God's word to guide.
Understanding there is nothing we can hide.
We can trust him as we accept his love.
Living each day fully as if it is a treasure trove.
Sent down to us from God above.

BOUNDARIES

Boundaries are necessary to set.
Lest we forget,
They are wonderful protection.
We need to provide a connection.
A way to show where we begin and end,
And a chance to forever mend.
An unintentional crossing
Of boundaries, tossing,
A roadblock in our way.
With boundaries, we can say,
I am sorry and regret,
Those boundaries weren't met.

ANTICIPATION

I feel a great anticipation in this season.
A spirit reawakening as Jesus's gift is the reason.
Lent is a time of reflection.
Giving up an unnecessary action,
Like watching TV or spending time,
Or energy in anything not a prime
Directive from my higher power.
God, who is the tower.
Above all else in my life of faith.
Bible passages beginning with "thus saith".
The Lord is my focus, no other locus,
For the anticipation I feel.
He is the Divine reel,
In the "movie" of my life of anticipation.

UNWAVERING FAITH

When I waver, I lose direction.
I feel at loose ends, without protection.
I long for a faith that is steady,
Unchanging in force.
It is the faith that steers my course.
Keeping my steps from faltering,
As God prevents me tottering.
My life in disarray.
If in my faith, I sway.
It is unwavering faith that will stay,
With me as a guide through my day.
Protecting me in every way.

DEDICATION

It is in dedication that one can find meaning.
Giving evidence of the life to which, we are leaning.
There are many forms of dedication.
It can be to a person, profession, or even a location.
Giving your all to whatever you are dedicated to.
Knowing that in the passion you feel, you do.
Everything you know to advance,
Fulfillment with all that you chance,
To be able to bring to fruition.
What dedication has placed you in position.
Accomplishing so much more,
Then you thought heretofore

PEACE

I'm not sure I understood the meaning of peace before.
Thought that it meant war and conflict would be no more.
No longer do I believe peace is a lack of conflict.
Nor is it the passing of a government edict.
Declaring everyone must get along.
No distinction between the weak and strong.
When Jesus said, "my peace I leave with you",
It was a different peace than the world could do.
The knowledge that He is always with you,
Through the good and bad, happy and sad.
It is the belief that God will provide relief.
Shelter and rest in His loving arms,
Keeping us safe from all the worlds' harms.

FAITH

Belief without proof; unmeasurable but powerful.
Life is enriched by faith, helping me to feel hopeful.
If I have the faith of a mustard seed,
That would be all I would need,
To move a mountain is what the Bible says.
I can indeed look back on all the ways,
My faith has aided me in facing many trials.
I have traveled a great distance in miles.
My faith journey over the years
Has helped to conquer my fears.
Knowing that each year my faith increases
Until the day that my life on earth ceases.

OVERCOMING

This season that we are in makes us look at all our sin.
Overcoming death, Jesus shows us how to live.
We lose ourselves by learning how to give.
In overcoming our own selfishness and pride.
In overcoming the world's belief in self, we now provide.
What we have with others, expecting no reward.
We are lifted in our giving looking forward,
To that time in the future when we meet our Lord.
Our savior who teaches us to forgive and live.
A life of overcoming our own trials to give.
Honor and glory to God as we perceive.
What Jesus, in overcoming, allowed us to receive.

DISCERNMENT

Discernment is so much more than understanding.
I am often in a situation that requires handling.
Letting go of my inability to correctly discern,
To a greater power so I can learn.
All the perception, insight, and deep listening
Discernment encompasses as I am christening.
A new relationship with God to establish.
An ability to discern as I wish.
Knowing that it is in discernment, I grow.
My faith, I don't just believe, I know.

INTENTIONALITY

The word "intentionality" has struck a chord with me of late.
We are not designed by God with the intention to hate.
When I state that it is my intention, I mean aim.
Now I am focused on another synonym, not quite the same.
I look at how I dwell on an objective.
Am I fully focused on what I hope I have achieved?
Or am I hoping that in what I do, my conscience is relieved?
I think of my actions as a Christian and ask.
Do my actions accomplish the task?
Is the intentionality of my actions to seek?
Approval of others, trying to speak,
Words that please God and others, too.
Failing to realize it is impossible to do.
We may fool others, but not God who.
Knows the intentionality of our actions and still.
Provides a way to do His Will.

UNITY OF VOICE

We can live,
Because we know how to give.
Or we can die,
Because we failed to try.
It is a choice.
We can use our voice,
To speak out,
And maybe shout.
Why can't you see?
What together we can be.
If we speak in unity,
Going forward into infinity.

THE JOURNEY

The start of the journey was a difficult trek.
One day I was excited, the next day a wreck.
I would take one step forward and two steps back.
I found it hard to stay on track.
Somehow, I would focus on my lack,
And fail to try another tack.
In the middle of the journey, I developed some skills.
I was able to recognize the importance of my pills.
To help me in my journey over the hills,
And finding a path where each step fills.
All I have lost along the way and the many spills,
I have taken this bipolar journey and wills,
Me to continue and never give up my life.
As I have encountered many days of strife,
The last part of my journey, I can now reflect.
On what I have gained, and maybe, deflect,
My focus is away from what I have lost.
Choosing to ignore the substantial cost.

FREEDOM

I have often wondered what being truly free means.
Is it being able to do anything I want?
What happens when doing what I want affects others?
Have I taken away their freedom?
I believe freedom involves choices.
The choices I make have consequences.
Do I accept the consequences of my choices?
Where does my freedom end and yours begin?
Will I ever truly understand freedom?

STORMS

I sit and watch the sky darken.
I know that in that moment I should harken,
To the warning in the sound of thunder.
As the storm prepares to plunder,
And possibly do so much damage in its path,
To deliver a large amount of wreckage in its wrath.
But when that storm suddenly leaves,
The earth itself receives.
A beautiful awakening and awareness
Of God's continuing nearness.
As we witness the rainbows and dew,
That serves to remind us of the power only you,
Our God can provide as we take each day in our stride.
Often forgetting in our busy lives,
The wonder that in the storms God revives.

MOMENTS

Our life is filled with many moments, some good and some bad.
However, we view them, be glad they were had.
A moment in time can be so sublime, but we must remember.
That even though we cannot stay there, time does not surrender.
The moments we capture, attempting to hold onto the rapture.
We feel in that moment, so our mind develops some good memories.
To hold closely to us since life offers us few guaranties,
Of peaceful, quiet, restful moments.

TIME

Time is hard to grasp.
It passes too fast, not seeming to last,
Or it passes so slowly, we fail to notice fully.
All that's happened in a day,
Or enjoy it in every way.

FORGIVENESS

Sometimes, as I walk along a certain path.
I may stop and reflect on the moment I felt such wrath.
I am reminded once again of the hurt I felt.
When I was judged, I felt my confidence melt.
I have Bipolar, but I am not my illness.
It is only part of my road to wellness.
Then, I realize that all my anger,
Will only hurt me, if I allow it to linger.
I choose forgiveness to heal myself.
I let my anger turn from self,
And others, forgiveness filling my heart.
On this path, a new course I will chart.
Reminding myself, I am forgiven.
Therefore, I need to forgive.

GRATITUDE

All the times I have felt joy,
Are times I push away all situations that serve to annoy.
I only look at everything as a positive.
No longer dwelling on the negative.
I have a heart filled with gratitude.
Finding myself with a much better attitude.
All my complaints and grumblings
Turn into very distant mumblings.
So much gratitude in my heart.
There is nothing to make me part,
With these feelings, thinking with a start.
Why haven't I always felt gratitude in my heart?

REMEMBER WHEN

Often, I have heard this phrase,
Remember when hula hoop was all the craze,
Remember when summer passed in a haze,
And we were back to the good old school days.
Remember when we would shout.
Wanting to be heard when we were out and about.
Remember when life seemed so easy.
So carefree and almost breezy.
It is fun to remember when.
But this is now and not then.
Memories are good and can be a blast,
If you remember they are in the past.

*BE STILL

As I grow older, being still makes sense.
When I am still, life seems less tense.
Until recently I have failed to understand.
Constant motion gets out of hand.
I fail to stop and feel the awe.
Each new day brings with it all I saw.
The words "be still" are softly whispered in my ear.
I have never heard it sound so clear.
It is difficult for me to be still.
But when I am, I understand God's will.

WISHES

Sometimes a wish seems unattainable, unreachable.
A wish can also be sustainable and valuable.
It can reflect an unrealized dream or scheme,
That may hold you back, stuck in a theme.
If you don't take a good look and pray,
And listen carefully to what God has to say.

BELIEF

We wonder why we are here, not there.
We think about our identity.
Considering if there is an entity,
Who brought us into being.
Why we are not seeing,
All the reasons for the seasons.
For why we have life with strife.
For why we feel relief.
When we have our belief,
A belief in a higher power
Without any need to cower.

TREASURE

What I treasure most is time!
Time spent with family and friends.
It is the treasure that God gave.
Time for me to store up and save.
Memories that will never fade.
No need for me to seek accolade.
I know that I would not trade.
The treasure of the time I have right now.
No focus on what I must do or even how,
I need to spend this treasured time.
Spending time, experiencing peace that is sublime.
I cannot think of any other way,
Or anything else that I could say.
Your treasure reveals your heart.
So today, please make a start.
Consider what treasure you want to impart,
To all those you hold dear in your heart.

LOSS

Dwelling on my loss in my mind
Many gains I will fail to find.
Blocking out the memories of time spent,
Of all the support that was lent.
So many blessings will be lost.
There will be an enormous cost.
In my loss, so many gains God will toss.
Allowing me to understand that in letting go,
My faith will continue to grow.
The gain will far outweigh the loss for me.
I will be able to see.
Using all the lessons learned,
Having images of those I lost to be burned,
Into the recesses of my mind.
No longer allowing my loss to bind.

LISTENING

I do think listening is a lost art.
We want to talk, not listen with our heart.
Jesus listens, encouraging us to start.
We need to listen to God and others.
Treating all as sisters and brothers.
With one father in Heaven, we are blessed,
Because He wants what is best.
If we listen and obey,
He will lead the way.
First, we need to be listening.
That will be the beginning.
A daily walk with God,
With His encouragement and nod.

WHAT WILL DEFINE ME

I have a few characteristics that may define me.
I am height challenged, getting more so with each passing year.
I can disappear in a crowd, making me difficult to see.
But I do possess a loud voice so others can hear.

I've worn glasses for most of my life, especially when I drive.
I have no depth perception as I have only one good eye.
I have had some close calls, but God kept me alive.
For which I am thankful as I am unready to bid good-bye.

There is one characteristic that I hope will define me.
It is the one that took me into nursing, caring.
Seeing what is needed by another and sharing.
Hoping that in the actions I take, it is a Christian they see.

I don't think money or fame should define me.
It is a joyful life I hope others see.
I have peace as a child of God, knowing He is always there.
Ready to comfort, His presence to share.

SEARCHING

Searching for meaning and my place meant many lost years.
Standing alone, not seeking guidance and shedding many tears,
I reached a place in my life where everything changed.
I met my Lord and Savior, and all things were rearranged.

My searching didn't stop, and I didn't become complacent.
My searching led to growing as I realized why God sent.
His Son into the world to die upon the cross.
A relationship with God to reestablish after our loss.

Searching became easier as I learned to pray.
Giving up my will so God could have His say.
Allowing Him to lead in every way.
His perfect Will would save my day.

Searching will not give me all the answers.
Questions will continue as I search,
For the answers far out of my reach.
Knowing only God can provide those answers.

IMPETUOUSNESS

Impetuousness is hard to control.
One of my bipolar symptoms which take a toll.
If I am unaware, jumping in without a thought,
Weaving a web where I am perilously caught.

It can cause me to speak before I think.
Relationships brought to the brink,
Of destruction or an indefinite separation,
It would be difficult to have reparation.

Impetuousness can get me in a financial mess.
Trouble with losses substantial, I confess.
It can put me in a dangerous position.
Proceeding amidst an unsafe condition.

Impetuousness cannot excuse my actions.
I must accept responsibility for transactions,
Made in the past so I can learn from my mistakes.
No matter how long it takes.

DEVELOPING

Matthew 7:7 "Ask, and it will be given to you. Seek, and you will find. Knock, and the door will be opened to you."

WISDOM

Some say wisdom comes with age.
I don't quite agree as wisdom may be the stage,
In life where knowledge and experience intervene.
Allowing our life to unfold like a scene.
Where we are acting the part of the wise,
Not sure how convincing we are as we see with surprise.
Age and wisdom are not mutually exclusive.
Wisdom can remain somewhat elusive.
Even at an age where we should be wise,
We find that age and wisdom do not have ties.
Binding them together in a tight vise.
Keeping us from planning in a way that is concise.
Wisdom is much more than learning and knowledge.
Age and experience can provide a wedge.
All these parts together can lead to wisdom, not as a whole,
Add in God and the Bible, where we develop a soul.

DELIGHT

What a wonderful word is the word delight!
I think my definition would be to bask in the light.
The dictionary defines it as highly pleasing.
Often, I find delight in nature as I sit there gazing.
Wonder and delight complement each other.
The look on the face of a new mother.
First steps and each new discovery as our children grow,
Allow for momentary delight as we know.
The days will come when they leave home,
Starting a new life of their own.
Our delight will be revisited in our grandchildren one day.
We will probably show our delight in a different way.

NEW BEGINNINGS

Every day is a new beginning.
Letting go of yesterday, allowing an ending.
Viewing each day as a new day.
Can be a blessing to live a different way.
I have no baggage to weigh me down.
No longer needing to wear a frown.
A smile on my face to let light shine forth.
Setting up a new course to find my true north.
An example I learned from a special person in my life,
Who always used her humor to battle any strife.
Today is a new beginning to greet this day.
I will let God lead my way.

A BLESSING IN OBEDIENCE

Obedience requires you to listen and hear.
Doing those things without fear.
In our actions we show faith and trust,
As we perform those actions, we know we must.
Willing ourselves to heed another's voice.
Acting as if we had no choice.
Not realizing that obedience brings a blessing.
Sometimes, it is just the lessening,
Of our own anxieties and fears.
God taking it on and drying our tears.
Amid our troubles, we may find,
Obedience may bring us peace of mind.

GRACE

This five-letter word impacts me in a powerful way.
It's the first thing I experience at the start of my day.
I can rest in the reality of God's saving Grace.
Knowing that I am encompassed by God's embrace.
I can do nothing to deserve it, just accept.
Allowing all I do through the day be kept,
In God's will to follow the path of the disciples.
Keeping to the teaching of Jesus and the principles,
He lived in his time on earth.
His humble birth to parents who put fear aside.
Showing by their actions they would abide.
All the challenges involved in raising the Son of God.
God's Grace reflected at the birth on Mary's face,
After nine months of awaiting her son to show his face.

GRACE AND MERCY

If you had a coin, grace and mercy would be opposites.
Both would show the love in which God delights.
In grace, God gives us what we don't deserve.
If we accept, we desire to serve.
In mercy, God does not give us what we do deserve.
What a gift that is when we can observe.
It sometimes takes life to throw us a curve,
Before we realize the value of these gifts
And the many ways, in grace and mercy, God uplifts.
All the healing provided for those rifts.
A life without grace and mercy would leave us bereft.

THE ROAD AHEAD

At times, it is hard to see the road ahead.
It is obscured in our hearts and head,
By the overwhelming grief we feel.
As we allow that grief to steal,
All the good memories we have.
We need to balance the grief with joy as we pave,
A new course to travel in this life.
Without you here by our side, facing strife.
We know you are in a better place by far.
Not here on Earth as we are.

ENCOURAGEMENT

As I consider how to help others, encouragement is the word.
Coming to my mind for I know that it has brought me forward.
When I have been feeling down, encouragement has lifted me.
As I have been encouraged over the years, I can see.
The words used to encourage me have been the greatest gift.
The encouragement of a friend has caused me to shift.
My views and actions away from a negative drift.
Therefore, I will help others through encouragement.
I will use my words as a testament,
Of what God has done for me in using others to bring.
Encouragement to me, allowing me to cling,
To those positive words, encouraging me to shout and sing.

PERCEPTION

I learned a long time ago that my perception can err.
I may perceive a situation as I plan to show I care,
When all that was asked of me was just to listen.
Not to plan a massive mission or even envision
A path forward, guided by my perception.
I remember, in psychology, looking at a picture,
As well as listening to a lecture.
Demonstrating how wrong my perception could be.
Now I wait before I act, choosing to see,
Whether my perception is rightly guiding me.

INTEGRITY

A word used infrequently today,
The concept of integrity has many parts, I say.
Giving my word and keeping it is one way,
To show integrity and, if I am honest, I pray.
I walk the talk to show integrity every day.
I do unto others as God does to me.
Not passing judgement or failing to see
Another in need of kindness, being free,
To give of myself and never flee.
From a difficult situation, bending my knee,
To pray God gives me the strength, that is the key.

SEEKING STILLNESS

I find myself seeking stillness throughout my day.
Knowing that in stillness, I can find my way.
The verse I love says "Be still and know that I am God".
In the stillness I can feel His presence and His nod.
Letting me rest and renew myself as I follow.
Allowing me to show a faith that is not hollow.
In constant motion, I cannot think.
All my actions seem to pass in a blink.
But in stillness, time slows.
As God continually shows,
What happens when stillness grows,
And faith in action flows.

SURRENDER

I have learned that surrender is a positive view.
It is not negative, if you act on its' cue.
I held on to things too much in the past.
Causing certain bad feelings to last.
I found freedom in surrender.
A freedom to be tender,
With me and others who judged my actions.
Blaming my diagnosis for some of my reactions.
I can surrender and forgive past mistakes.
As I learn and discover how much it takes,
Away from my life and any joy I feel.
If I don't surrender, allowing myself to be real.

RECONCILIATION

What a wonderful word and action is reconciliation.
Letting go of past mistakes to lead to a cessation,
Of all the bad feelings and a fracture.
In our relationship, send our feelings out to pasture.
Allowing a healing to take place, showing God's grace.
Sometimes there is reconciliation in a whole nation.
What a blessing that can be!
Especially for the world to see.
Knowing that in reconciliation, a relationship can form.
Much different from the norm
That existed in the past.
Hoping reconciliation brings a relationship that will last.

A PLAN

I start each day by planning.
Not always sure which steps I can
Put into place to accomplish all.
I need to do to, so I don't fall,
Behind in seeing my plan fulfilled,
And feeling like I have filled.
Every moment in my day,
Making my plan complete this way.
It is only lately I've come to realize.
The plan I have is not the one, I surmise.
The plan that God has in mind for me.
I rearrange my plan to the one that is meant to be.

PROMISES

Promises are the words you say as a pledge,
To do what you will as you acknowledge,
The needs of another or even yourself.
Keeping your word shows integrity of self.
A promise should not be easily made.
Since, not following through, we trade.
Our worth, our words shown to be untrue.
Our promises will be empty, without substance.
No one will believe and take a chance,
On believing our promises.

ASSURANCE

I have the assurance that in each day.
God will be with me as I display,
The assurance my faith gives me today.
I have the assurance that there is no way.
God will not choose to play.
A part in my life to keep me from the fray.
I have the assurance He will never betray,
Or lead me astray.
I have the assurance of His love,
And the many blessings in His treasure trove.
I have the assurance of His peace,
That gives my life a new lease.
I have the assurance that his presence,
In my life will never cease.

PRIDE

A very difficult subject is pride.
It can sometimes override.
Our best intentions to make a wise decision,
Often clouding our vision.
Pride can lead us to be unforgiving.
We can cease to be people intent on giving.
Leaving us no longer living
A Christian life, focused on others.
We start thinking of all the bothers.
In our current situation pride takes over.
We may try to place a cover.
Denying our pride is the reason.
Leaving us in a very dry season.
God may be teaching us a lesson.
Showing the truth of the adage to all.
"Pride goes before the fall".

ADVERSITY

Some believe that adversity is bad.
I believe that a life lived without adversity is sad.
I can't think you can live a life,
Without any adversity or strife.
There would be nothing to challenge you.
Would you have a point of view?
I can only see a lukewarm person.
Who lives without any passion.
Who goes along day by day,
Not showing a different way.
Remaining the exact same person today,
As he/she was yesterday.
With adversity is a strengthened resolve,
To see things through and solve,
The results of adversity as they evolve.

CHALLENGES

I need challenges in my life, I know.
It is those challenges that make me grow.
I may complain and refrain,
From acknowledging how important,
Challenges are so I don't stay content.
Flowing along in a bubble
Not letting any of the rubble
Affect me in any way through my day.
Continuing in the exact same path without
Any changes brought on by challenges about
Who I am or who I hope to be.
Always being the same me!

WEARY

In my mind, I find.
I feel so weary.
Sad times also make me teary,
To feel weary is to be beyond tired.
Very often, finding myself mired
In negative thoughts.
Thoughts which never brought,
Me any relief, even with a rest that is brief.
I can only lift my weariness,
By turning to God in His righteousness.
Remembering, it is He who can carry,
Me away every time I feel weary.
I will dwell in His strength,
Through the length
Of all my days on Earth.
Experiencing a rebirth.

HEALING

Healing takes a great deal of time.
I wish that my life could be sublime.
Without the need for healing
Always experiencing a good feeling.
Healing does not occur overnight.
It often requires a dedicated fight.
A purpose for healing kept in our sight.
Healing comes in very small increments.
Not without voicing many laments.
Healing doesn't make us whole.
God is the only one who can lift the toll.
Making all things right in our soul.

RESURRECTION

Each year, as Easter approaches, I reflect,
On the meaning of resurrection to detect.
What does it mean to me at this point in my life?
Rising again in faith? Or revival from strife?
The resurrection of Christ frees me from sin.
But it is not the whole story for I have a pin.
That states Christ lives again in me.
As I become the child of God, He wants me to be.
There is a resurrection happening right now.
As we are challenged to learn how
To establish a new normal way to live.
Post pandemic, letting go of loss as we forgive.

CELEBRATION OF LIFE

With a smile, I choose to embrace.
This day in God's saving grace,
Jesus took my sins, endured disgrace.
Conquered death, leaving no trace,
Of unforgiveness for our human race.
Today is a celebration of life as we brace,
For any trials ahead, knowing we have,
A place in Heaven that Jesus will save.
Knowing that all we crave
Is connection to God while on this sod.

JUDGEMENT

Images of judgement are easy to see.
The finger pointed directly at me.
A head shaking in disappointment, and a plea.
Eyes looking sorrowfully at what has come to be.
Good and bad judgement are often examined.
But do we fail to see all the steps combined?
What we need to take to break
A cycle of bad judgement in our life?
Reason, emotion, knowledge of how to be a good wife,
Or husband, parent or child or knowing when to be.
A listener, seeker, attentive, or active and forceful as we
Strive for good judgement if we are alive.

*ASK, SEEK, FIND

Who do I ask?
Who do I seek?
Who do I find?
What do I ask?
What do I seek?
What do I find?
Those questions changed my life.
As a child, it was my mother I asked.
Often to seek understanding
Finding guidance and love.
She demonstrated God's love.
I found purpose, faith, and hope.
In my chosen profession of nursing,
I asked instructors and fellow nurses.
Who mentored me as they guided,
My path to become a better nurse.

IN THE QUIET OF
THE MORNING

In the early morning hours, I hear the birds singing.
The noise is dampened down, no telephones ringing.
It is in the quiet of the morning that I can wonder.
All the questions in my life to ponder.
I can spend time alone with my thoughts.
Not dwelling on the many aughts,
In my life I enjoy my quiet time.
I can realize it is no crime to enjoy my quiet time.
In the quiet of the morning, I spend time with nature.
As I thank God for all He does to nurture
In the quiet of the morning, I spend time by myself.
Understanding the need to care for self.
Enjoying the quiet of the morning to start a new day.
Holding all the noise and activity at bay.

SUCCESS IN LIFE

To some, success means having more of everything.
More money, more power, more property to bring,
Before others to cause them to envy or covet.
Others see success is how life is lived, a net,
Of positive experiences to show a well lived life.
The overcoming of all the difficulties and strife.
I view success in life as allowing God to use.
The gifts He gives me to honor Him and fuse,
His image with mine so I can truly be His.
Knowing that success is living in His image.

BALANCE

The older I am, the more important balance becomes.
Balance encompasses many things: electrolytes, hormones.
The ability to stay upright when aboard a moving ship,
Or in changing positions, even though very slight.
In my journey, balance means intentionally noting,
When my mood is radically changing.
Reaching for the sky or hitting rock bottom.
I must take steps to address these changes.
Using coping techniques, offering many ranges,
Of effectiveness so a balance is reestablished.
A balance between mania and depression.
A balance to continue a healthier life.

EVALUATING

Ecclesiastes 3:1-8 "There is an occasion for everything and a time for every activity under heaven: a time to give birth and a time to die; a time to plant and a time to uproot; a time to kill and a time to heal; a time to tear down and a time to build; a time to weep and a time to laugh; a time to mourn and a time to dance; a time to throw stones and a time to gather stones; a time to embrace and a time to avoid embracing; a time to search and a time to count as lost; a time to keep and a time to throw away; a time to tear and a time to sew; a time to be silent and a time to speak; a time to love and a time to hate; a time for war and a time for peace."

TODAY

Today is a new day,
Amazing in every way.
I can choose what I want to do.
I can choose where I want to go.
I can choose who and what I want to know.
I can also choose if I want to grow.
In faith, knowledge, wisdom, and how I treat others,
I can treat them as sisters and brothers.
I can look beyond their outward appearance,
And understand, with strict adherence,
The meaning of the word Christian.
Today, spreading Jesus and his gift is the mission.

CLOUDS

When my children were young
We played a game naming animals found among
The shapes of clouds we saw as we traveled by car.
Providing entertainment, especially when we were going far.
I have always found clouds thought provoking.
A slew of emotions often evoking.
The science behind their formation can't explain,
What causes our tendency to complain,
About those gray days we tend to blame.
On those clouds that provide a frame,
Blocking out the sun,
And depriving us of our fun.
Next time you see a cloud.
Don't join the crowd,
In blaming the clouds and weather
On all the emotions, we hold together.

RANDOM THOUGHTS

Many times, throughout my day,
Random thoughts come my way.
The thought may be something new,
Or an old thought out of the blue.
It may be a thought about a person from my past.
Someone I am led to reach out to at last.
Finding to my surprise, I was the person.
They needed to hear from, providing a lesson,
Those random thoughts might not be random at all.
They might be a reminder from God to heed his call.

WANDERING WITH WONDER

I have spent a big part of my life wandering from place to place.
Finding myself for the past twenty years staying in the same space.
Looking back often in wonder at the places my wandering took me.
Hoping soon to revisit one of my most favorite places and see.
How time has changed it since it has been thirty-six years.
My age is now more advanced, and my life has changed gears.
I was a young mother then, now I am a grandmother.
I think maybe my wandering with wonder provides another,
Reason for keeping me looking younger than my age.
Sometimes making it difficult for others to gauge.
The years I have spent wandering with wonder,
Until the time I am called to go up yonder.

OPPORTUNITY

Suddenly, one day I was deep in thought.
I considered what opportunity had brought.
I had a purpose in my life.
I had the opportunity to be a wife.
Every time I took a step, enabled to see,
An opportunity placed before me.
My faith grew as I knew,
Who placed that opportunity in my path.
Many times, missing those opportunities God hath,
Given to me if I did the math,
I would surely see how great my life would be.
Addressing every opportunity God gives to me.

STORIES

I believe it is in my story that I find a way,
Of handling my worries as they replay,
All the events throughout my day.
Some are good; some are bad.
Some are happy; some are sad.
Woven into a tapestry, all the moments I've had.
Creating a whole picture of my life story.
Praying that I am giving God the glory.
Honoring Him with my life's story.
As I use my story to display,
All the many events, God has put into play,
To be the potter of my clay.

DISTRACTIONS

There are so many distractions throughout my day.
Making it difficult to bypass the roadblocks in my way,
As I try to progress in becoming who.
God wants me to be and to do,
His will, not letting distractions play.
A part in my relationship so I can display.
Christian maturity as I journey in my faith life.
Knowing a Christian life does not preclude strife.
Distractions are Satan's way of breaking the bond,
To change the relationship of which I am fond.
Distractions take away the time I spend with God.
While I am present here on Earth's sod.

COINCIDENCES

As I reflect on my life, I find an overlap,
Of coincidences that seemed to wrap,
Around those times of stress and upheaval.
Allowing circumstances to avail.
An opportunity to overcome,
Any situation, preventing a bad outcome.
Coincidences are a divine intervention.
A way to demonstrate God's intention.
Making my life less tense.
Looking through a better lens.
Showing me a "God" wink,
That is what I choose to think.

MOUNTAINS AND VALLEYS

I love mountains, but feeling as if I am on top
Of a mountain can be an expression of mania.
I feel like I can do anything with nothing to stop.
I am no longer in control as it is mania
That controls me as I no longer see
Any boundaries that will protect me.

Valleys are the times of depression.
Where everything weighs me down,
I greet each day with a frown.
It is a time when I question
What is the reason for my being?
As everything good I am no longer seeing.

God has enabled me to lower the mountains
And raise the valleys to allow me to sustain.
Knowing that in His Presence, I can feel grounded,
My life forever founded on the truth of his existence.

DREAMS REALIZED

In my life, many dreams have been realized.
A dream came into focus and crystallized.
I became a nurse, a wife, a mother, and a grandmother.
I have lived a very full life with no other
Unrealized dreams causing me regret.
God gave me opportunities that at times I met,
Seizing the moment to realize a dream.
God gave me the strength to see and deem
I had the ability to take it in hand and seem
To wholly realize that dream.

MIRACLES

I believe in miracles because I have seen them.
Sometimes, it may be difficult to learn.
A miracle has happened because we are unaware.
When we pay attention, we know how much care
God has for us in every little and big event.
He never leaves, he is always present.
Pray with belief that a miracle will happen.
We may not remember, but with paper and pen,
We can recognize and be a witness to his care and love.
Knowing he is always with us, not just above.

WINTER

A time of reflection is winter to me,
Wondering always what will come to be.
Moving forward in my life without regret,
Not allowing my mind to fret.
Focusing on now and what is yet to come.
Enjoying the warmth and comfort of my home.
Welcoming the cooler temperatures now.
Planning on reading and learning how
To relax in the present time.
As I realize putting myself first isn't a crime.
Winter can be the best of seasons,
A time to think about the many reasons
Life is good, despite the trials.
Time yet to travel more miles.
My life journey is only half done.
Many lessons have been hard won.

SPRING

The promise of new life comes with spring.
Birds chirping, trees blooming add to my days a zing.
Longer days, warmer temps, and new growth bring
A glow with the contemplation of new adventures.
Allowing me to reach out and sample new textures.
Recognizing in myself a new openness to observe,
Not trying to continue my old ways to preserve
What is in the past and try to make it last.
Now witnessing how life can be a blast.
Spring with all its newness adding wonder,
Causing new ideas and ventures to ponder.

COME NEAR AND REST

I have always been on the move, finding it hard to be still.
Before I was diagnosed as Bipolar, I thought I was doing God's Will.
Constantly moving and doing, I failed to rest.
In this long journey, I will have to contest
That I was doing His Will by always moving.
Instead, I was somehow proving
God wanted me to come near and rest.
I had not listened to His Voice to provide for my best.
When I come near and listen as I rest, I feel His presence.
He wants nothing more from me than to sense
The closeness of my walk with God
Can happen best when I come near and rest.

A MOTHER'S TRIBUTE

In every day, we can give tribute,
To Mothers who touched our lives without repute.
Who helped us to find our way.
Led us in actions and words to portray.
The kind of people we would strive to be.
Enabling the world to see
Love of God shown through the love our mothers gave.
Many times, our lives to save,
Preventing us from being a slave to sin
A Christian life to win!

A FATHER'S LOVE

A father's love is a wonder to behold.
As his arms, lovingly enfold,
His children, tending to any woe.
Protecting them from every foe.
A father's love can serve to glimpse.
The love of God, but it will never eclipse.
The love God showed by giving His Son.
To take on our sin so we won,
Redemption from our sin.
Reunited with God, Our Father, again.

CENTERED

Centered is a word I have come to love.
I feel a balance as never before.
I accept myself as I am, with some knowledge at my core,
That I am loved by my savior up above.

God is at the center of my universe.
It is His love quoted in a Bible verse.
So great He sent His Son
To show His love, allowing His will to be done.

Centered in the word of God.
Feeling His presence and His love
Waiting patiently for His nod
To do His will as sent from above.

Centered in knowing I have a precious gift.
A life worth living as I shift,
From looking within and judging my sin,
To the belief that, in the end, God will win.

Centered amid other believers,
Who are the receivers of God's word.
As they carry His word to others in need.
Establishing a mission and planting a seed.

Centered in a new season where God is the reason.
I am incredibly blessed with good mental health,
And a healthy body with such a wealth,
Of spiritual enlightenment and discernment.

DESIRES

No matter where you are in your life, you have desires.
If you don't, there seems to be no passion or fires.
Burning in your heart to fuel a start to living.
Every day is as if it is your first and feeling a thirst.

Desires to quench that thirst.
Desires to see life as an adventure, but first.
You must look at your past, present, and possible future.
Seeing clearly who, what, and where you are.

Desires to fuel the energy you will need,
To do the things you want and succeed.
Knowing all you have is a gift from God.
The desires you have are His nod.

Desires may be a way to honor God.
A passion to live a Christian life.
With God at the center to help with any strife.
Waiting patiently to hear His word and get His nod.

*TOO FAST A TIME

Each year, time speeds up
Nothing seems to hinder the filling of my cup.
I have too many unfinished projects
Too many unfulfilled dreams, no prospects
Of reaching a goal, meeting expectations no one respects

Too fast a time to enjoy.
Too fast a time to employ.
Never managing to treasure joy.

Taking time to sit and rest.
Is not something that I do best.
I may try to slow down time,
To seize a moment in my prime.
Knowing that taking moments for myself is no crime.

Too fast a time to enjoy.
Too fast a time to employ.
Never managing to cherish joy.

TIME PASSES

Time passes, seconds, moments, and days.
I sit and count the many ways.
Time passes, many activities are on display.
I look back, images in my mind to play.

Time passes, everything changes.
Many wonderful places that nature rearranges.
Time passes, sometimes with wonder,
As I press forward to look yonder.

Time passes, a moment becomes a day.
A day becomes a year as time slips away.
Time passes, nothing could be gained,
If you tried in vain and bargained.

Time passes, until there is a lack.
Sometimes as time passes, you lose track.
You can try a different tack.
But time passes, and you can never get it back.

THE LIGHT OF DAY

Seeing things clearly requires the light of day.
Darkness can obscure impediments in the way.
The light of day brings perspective.
Not always providing a good directive.

In warmer seasons, the light of day lasts longer still.
Adding hours to the day, reflecting light on the windowsill.
You would think this increased light,
Would serve to confuse about night.

In colder seasons, the light of day shrinks away.
Darkness increases and can betray,
Our senses in such a way
That lack of energy comes into play.

It is in the balance of light and dark.
We can leave our mark.
Light can lift us while it is dark.
Can makes us lose our spark.

NO BOUNDS

There are those who know no bounds.
They may constantly make the rounds.
Leaving nothing in their wake,
So much more to take.

Always on the move, as they try to prove.
No bounds are needed for them.
Making sure there are no grounds,
For others to insist upon these bounds.

No bounds to stop or maybe drop,
A subtle hint or request
Made at another's behest.
Bounds make a lot of sense.

Knowing no bounds can lead.
Many who are tempted to proceed.
Leading them into uncharted waters.
Hoping that their luck never falters.

FEELING

Proverbs 31:30 "Charm is deceptive, and beauty is fleeting, but a woman who fears the Lord will be praised."

BLESSINGS

All the blessings I received when first I believed.
The people I came to know; the places that I go.
Do wonderfully reveals the amazing way I feel.
When I understand the beautiful plan,
God has for me and the person I am to be.
Brought out by the blessings of He who made me.
I now see and now realize the incredible prize,
Of the many blessings of my life.
The blessing of being a wife.
The blessing of being a mother.
Knowing an opportunity like no other.
Thank you, God, for my belief,
That all you give me is a relief,
From the grief sometimes found in this world.
All the blessings unfurled.

*FEAR

Forever
Enveloping
Admiring
Reverence
We often view fear in a negative manner.
When this anagram could be put on a banner,
To put the word fear in a new perspective,
And show a different, positive reflective.
Way to consider how we view,
The many references to "fear of God" anew.

JOY

It is hard to imagine that one three letter word.
Could encompass what I feel with you in my life, Lord.
Joy in the bad times as well as the good.
It is more than just a mood.
The joy of life I feel helps me navigate my journey daily.
Bipolar can disrupt my life otherwise and rarely,
Take me down a road I don't want to go.
Especially in a situation where I don't say no.
Allowing the joy to dissipate and leave me,
In a place I don't want to be.
I will choose to experience joy every day,
And allow me to let joy lead the way.

LAUGHTER

What I remember most about those I have lost,
Is laughter amid all the accomplishments we boast.
The gatherings and memories of all the tall tales.
Recounted by my grandfather and most of the males.
Seeking to regale all the ladies present.
In many ways, asking them to consent,
To pull the legs of those who were younger.
Until the smell of food induced a hunger
For a while all talk was suspended.
And some of the stories were upended.
But always there were chuckles at the time,
When it was stated, they were hardly worth a dime.

HOPE

Hope is a four-letter word with a lot behind it.
There's a wonderful message that we often don't get.
A world with a lack of hope would be a dark place.
Somehow existing without God's Grace.
Hope allows a light in the darkness.
An ability to be transported to a place of lightness.
Without hope, there would be fear and sadness.
I know there would be an increase in mortality,
Because there would be a bitter reality.
With no recognition of a better tomorrow
All we would feel is a lot of sorrow,
Nothing to look forward to tomorrow.

RENEWAL

If I view each day as a new day,
I can arrange my life in a different way.
I can start anew with an uplifted view.
Feeling a renewal as I travel today.
Letting go of all that was yesterday.
I can embrace today when I let go.
Enabling myself to continue to grow.
Renewal provides me with hope.
I find myself more able to cope.
I am no longer in a mire of my own making.
Instead, I am now allowing God's taking,
Control in my renewal, becoming the me.
God wants me to be.

SERENITY

The word "serenity" trips off the tongue.
Providing a sense of peace for which I long.
Even the sound of the word has a calming effect,
In my life that allows me to perfect
A wonderful way to face every day.
I choose to be "serene" in the face of trouble.
It lets me erect a soothing bubble.
Surrounding myself with a protective layer.
Emerging from bad situations as a positive player.
Allowing a face of "serenity" to shine through,
As all the storms of life brew.

A FOND FAREWELL

My heart is no longer heavy,
As I know that you are no longer suffering.
I will miss you in our daily devotion time.
I can see you in my mind,
And know you are in my heart.
You were in my life from our first meeting.
September 1974, you welcomed me graciously.
I was blessed with two mothers,
Who, though different, were very alike in their faith.
I felt your love and welcome every day,
From that first meeting.
Your legacy is your love of God and family.

EMOTIONS

Ups and downs; happiness and sadness; elation and depression
Can be simultaneously present in every situation.
Trying to avoid feeling or emotions can't be done.
Emotions not dealt with means no one has won.
Viewing the experience of emotions as bad,
Leaves a feeling of being incredibly sad.
Finding a balance and enjoying the emotion
Can bring us peace, understanding the notion,
That life is a gift of good and bad to help us grow.
Knowing that in our growth, wisdom will come.
Until finally, we will go to our eternal home.

TOUCH

Learning about the world around us
Using the five senses God gave to focus.
Sight, smell, sound, taste, and touch
Provides a basis in which to couch.
All the knowledge of the world around.
What if we don't have sound?
Another sense will provide for this lack.
Although, loss of touch can set us back.
Not realizing how touch can nurture.
Having a big effect on our future
A lack of touch may cause us not to thrive.
Preventing us from feeling alive
We connect when we touch,
That connection provides us with so much.

GRIEF

I find myself feeling grief throughout my day.
Sometimes I can handle it and keep it away.
But now I know it is best to meet grief head on.
It will never be entirely gone.
It has been a month since yesterday.
Mama went to Heaven as she could not stay,
Her body and her will to live,
Meant she had no more time to give.
The grief she had at the loss of a son,
Deprived her of her joy and death won.
Now, in my loss, I will choose to joyfully dwell,
On all the shared times we had to fill.
Not letting the grief, I feel to kill,
My joy in living every day.
Keeping the grief at bay.

LETTING GO

I hold on tight to many things in my life,
As I strive to be the best wife.
Taking care of others in my own strength,
Finding as I do, it only adds to my day's length.
I come up short in my mind.
Because I know I will never find
The strength I need on my own.
I am learning to let go and disown.
The notion that I alone can do those things.
When I acknowledge I need help, it brings,
A sense of peace in letting go.
For I believe that God does know
The best plan for my life.
With His help, I can be the best wife.
I can do anything in His strength.
In letting go, there is a decrease in each day's length.

A CHANCE FOR RENEWAL

What I need is to see a new day change,
Then I can arrange my life a different way.
I can start anew with an uplifted view.
Feeling a renewal as I travel today.
Letting go of all that was yesterday.
I can embrace today when I let go.
Enabling myself to continue to grow.
Renewal provides me with hope.
I find myself more able to cope.
I am no longer in a mire of my own making.
Instead, I am now allowing God's taking.
Over the control in my renewal,
Becoming the me God wants me to be.

TEARS

I have always tried to hide my tears.
Unwilling to deal with my feelings and fears.
Wanting to keep everything inside.
Convincing myself that I could hide.
I could keep an outward show of strength.
Fooling only myself, going to the length,
Of putting a smile on my face.
Attempting to wipe off every trace.
Not viewing tears as God's plan,
To offer to each man and woman.
A needed release so sad feeling would cease.
Leaving a definite peace.

SHARING MY JOY
WITH OTHERS

Joy does not arise from what I have in life.
It comes from who is in my life.
What I have may give temporary happiness, never joy.
What I have not leaves me in sorrow and envy.
Those negative feelings take over to diminish joy.
My mother taught me not to seek joy.
It would come in my giving as I receive God's blessings.
It would be a lasting joy as I shared with others.
Joy would come from thanksgiving,
In all the times, good and bad, of my life.

EMPATHY, NOT SYMPATHY

I felt led to share this difference.
Though subtle, sometimes there is an inference,
That they are the same.
It is hard to find a way to change these differences to name.

Sympathy means recognizing sorrow.
Offering a comfort, unable to make a furrow,
In understanding to put yourself in the same place.
Placing limits on seeing the losses another can face.

Empathy means understanding.
Able to see where another is standing.
Similar experiences shared, able to see.
What the effect of those experiences would be.

I would choose empathy over sympathy any day.
My years of nursing have shown me the way.
Relating with empathy brings us closer together.
Better able the storms of life to weather.

DAYBREAK

Waking up to a new day!
Greeted by the sun rising.
Ready to get on my way.
Off to a family gathering, in the car cruising.

I am always grateful.
As I experience daybreak,
It can be truly beautiful.
A good start to a continuing trek.

Daybreak is the beginning.
You can decide how the day goes.
It can either have a happy or sad ending,
Depending on what one does.

Daybreak brings opportunities to see.
Deciding what the day will be.
You can be excited or depressed.
Allowing yourself to be stressed.

PROCESS OF RECOVERY

As a nurse, I have a certain definition.
Recovery is getting back to the previous position.
If you have a change in your health situation
Treatment and recovery are part of the plan of action.

Recovery is a broad subject to be addressed.
There are many parts to be stressed.
Looking at the steps needed.
A recovery can be completed.

Recovery is a process,
Not always a total success.
Times when a stage of recovery is met.
But total recovery, you may never get.

Recovery can give you inspiration.
Bringing you to a place with a new direction.
Finding a sense of self that is uplifted.
Areas to explore where you are gifted.

IN THE BLINK OF AN EYE

In the blink of an eye, years pass by
Trying not to look back with a sigh.
I find myself vexed,
As each decade blended into the next.

In what seemed like the blink of an eye
I went from a young woman to a mother.
Now from a mother to a grandmother
As so much time has gone by.

In the blink of an eye, I've spent,
Much time asking where the years went.
Now, finishing my seventh decade, I ponder.
All the time that has passed with wonder.

In the blink of an eye, days roll by even more.
Each day passes more quickly than before.
Sometimes shaking me to my very core,
Making sure there is nothing I ignore.

In the blink of an eye, my young grandchildren grow.
Now having a high school graduate too,
Taking the next step as to college she prepares to go.
Adding more experiences and things to know.

UNBURDENED

The burdens we carry, unwilling to share.
Often, not seeing how much God does care.
We try to handle them ourselves in pride.
Wanting to be strong, all weakness to hide.

Jesus tells us to lay down our burdens on Him.
He is the light of the world, but our light is dim.
Not understanding how many burdens He bares
We seem to hold on to all our cares.

If we trust in His love, unburdened are we.
Knowing that He will provide, and we will see,
An answer given and a way forward.
Unburdened with something to move toward.

Unburdened and feeling free with joy.
Untethered from a heavy weight, a buoy,
In the water bobbing up and down.
Unburdened and no longer wearing a frown.

AN UNRIVALED PEACE

It is only in the last few years that I have felt.
An unrivaled peace I can't explain.
A peace the world might disdain.
Provided by Jesus when at His altar, I have knelt.

A peace the world can never provide.
Even if it were to turn the tide,
Of hatred and despair,
That always seems so nearby.

An unrivaled peace no matter what may be.
It may be in the chaos of life where you can't see.
Why I have a peace that is surrounding me,
But the presence of Jesus is the key.

An unrivaled peace that no one can take away.
No matter what they do or say,
Or any of the destructive games they may play.
Because Jesus is the Truth and the Way.

FEELING FREE

To my surprise, I feel.
Unburdened by care.
Knowing the Lord is there.
Satan, my joy can't steal.

No longer to carry my woes.
Alone, combating numerous foes.
God steps in,
To forgive my sin.

Pride and selfishness put away,
Living in a new day.
Burdens no longer hold sway,
As Jesus is the Way.

Unburdened and feeling free.
Allowing joy to enter me.
Giving to God the glory and honor.
As life's difficulties I need not ponder.

GROWTH

Daniel 3:16-19 Shadrach, Meshach, and Abednego replied to the king, "Nebuchadnezzar, we don't need to give you an answer to this question. If the God we serve exists, then he can rescue us from the furnace of blazing fire, and he can rescue us from the power of you, the king. But even if he does not rescue us, we want you as king to know that we will not serve your gods or worship a gold statue you set up." Then Nebuchadnezzar was filled with rage, and the expression on his face changed toward Shadrach, Meshach, and Abednego. He gave orders to heat the furnace seven times more than was customary.

QUESTIONS

Sometimes things are not as they seem.
Often, they are really a dream.
Rarely can we see,
What our life will turn out to be.
There are so many choices.
Listening to too many voices.
Leads to a time of indecision and questions.
Asking about what ambitions and positions,
Leading to the best outcome.
One that would be most welcome.
Do I go or do I stay?
Can there be another way?
Can I manage a path that is in-between?
Is there another course yet unseen?
There are answers to these questions,
With possibilities for unending lessons.

BEGINNINGS

Lately, I look at each day as a new beginning.
As the sun rises, after a previous day ends,
I can choose to carry over past days' events.
I can let them go, so nothing prevents,
What I view as New Beginnings.
Not dwelling on other endings.
It can be a day of happiness,
Or a day of sadness.
I can choose to have a "glad" day,
Or I can wallow in a "bad" day.
I must remember what I choose.
Is not dependent on anything I lose.
I can be joyful in the now,
Allowing nature to wow.
So, here is to those New Beginnings,
And making a day's worth of happy endings.

RECYCLE

Recycle is a concept that many don't get.
Maybe the concept can be grasped on the Net.
Reuse and recycle have been popular in the past.
All sorts of ideas developed to make things last.
Now, with "throwaway" mentally, we fail,
To realize the future of our planet may derail.
We need to make a stand, or we may lose our land.
Recycle is no longer a choice; we must demand.
We must find our voice to save our land.
Recycle, reuse, repurpose must be our slogan.
Fighting for our earth's resources has begun.

FITTING IN

When I was young, fitting in was what I wanted most.
Just to be one of the crowds, and maybe boast,
About what I brought to the crowd I was fitting in.
Forgetting that pride and boasting were a sin.

As I grew older, fitting in was less important.
I am independent now, experiencing less want.
I could be with others or be alone.
Fitting in no longer set the tone.

As I age, fitting in takes a different stance.
I have a profession, talents, and gifts and a chance,
To make a difference in my world,
To make waves in the world like a flag unfurled.

At the start, fitting in was a way to mold.
What I had, what could be, I could be bold.
If it was what was expected of me,
That was how I let people see.

I could be forceful with my fists curled,
As everything around me twirled.
Fitting in, at the last, as my world passed.
Had been a way of life, from the present to the past.

REFRESHING RAIN

The sound of thunder warns of rain.
Gathering clouds fail to restrain,
The sudden heavy pelting drops of rain.
Providing refreshing water for crops to maintain.

Refreshing rain feeding the earth,
Protecting against a possible dearth.
Providing a balance between flood and drought.
Preventing an overabundance or an insufficient amount.

Refreshing rain brings a freshness to the air.
A feeling to which nothing else can compare.
There is a cleansing that the earth undergoes.
Bringing forth evidence of newness that grows

There is nothing better than to sit and read,
As the steady patter of the rain has freed.
Time from activities outside,
So, instead, I can choose in fantasy to hide.

MYSTERY OF LIFE

A precious gift to unlock.
There is much mystery,
Of life, in the direction we took.
What would become our life's history.

The mystery of life starts at conception.
Many factors intervene to change our direction.
We may start on a pathway that is a rocky one.
Do we change direction or continue until done?

The mystery of life to me is resilience.
We may give up, complain, or continue in silence.
Finding our strength in interaction,
With those who God sends to initiate action.

The mystery of life is love shared,
With family or friends with whom you've paired.
That love changes over the years.
It can grow or fade away with tears.

VALOR

Valor is a word not commonly heard,
Unless it is spoken while on a military base.
Reflecting a high honor in many cases.
An award for uncommon valor in a dangerous place.

Personal bravery is one definition I found.
I think of a fireman risking his/her life.
First responders and nurses holding their ground,
In these years of anxiety and strife.

Valor can also be found in anyone willing,
To speak out against injustice telling.
A truth that presents a risk of violence,
And imprisonment to silence.

Valor needs firmness and strength.
An ability to go to great lengths,
To rise above any danger seen.
Overcoming the losses that might have been.

SELF ESTEEM

How we look at ourselves is tied to self-esteem.
If we see qualities in ourselves that redeem,
We are more likely to have high self-esteem.

In comparison to others, we may deem.
We are less than others seem.
Leading us to have low self-esteem.

We may not think self-esteem matters,
But when we find it, it is tattered.
The joy we have in living scattered.

We can seem to have high self-esteem.
When we are pretending, living a dream,
Trying to be an essential part of the team.

Take an honest look at yourself to see.
If you are as authentic as you can be,
Able to clearly see that you are as good as me.

SOARING

At times, I feel as if I am soaring.
Which can cause a roaring,
Of warnings, coming to me.
It can be a foretelling of what will be.

Feeling as if I am soaring.
Does not have to be bad.
If it is not an indication of mania, pouring,
An artificial feeling, lasting briefly, as I become sad.

I visualize soaring on the wings of an Eagle, above high.
Carrying me over mountains, causing me to sigh,
If it is not a symptom of mania that shows.
Soaring brings me closer to the One who knows.

Soaring into the clouds.
Bringing me closer to God.
Rising high above the ground.
Praising God out loud.

MANY KINDS OF LOVE

There are so many kinds of love.
The kind God shows us from above.
An unconditional one, as a parent has for a child.
Even a child who chooses a path in life that is wild.

Romantic love that develops over time.
Into a lifelong love that will shine.
Bringing two people so close together,
They can act as one, all storms to weather.

Christian love between our sisters in Christ,
As we find a fellowship as disciples of Christ.
Challenged to live our life in a faith shown in love.
Following the guidance from above.

Familial love between brothers and sisters,
Varying in closeness but shown in trials.
As outside attacks, even with miles,
Arouses the protective traits of brothers and sisters.

*FACING FIRE WITH FAITH

When there is fire about a cause or job, passion exists.
Uncontrolled, that passion burns out.
Facing fire with faith sustains that passion.
Allowing that passion to continue and, maybe, grow.

When fire burns out of control, destroying,
It can lead to an experience of fear that is cloying.
Facing fire with faith offers impowering.
Overcoming all the loss.

When fire is used to temper steel, it strengthens.
Making that tool more useful and unbreakable.
Facing fire with faith also strengthens.
Our faith journey multiplies in strength.

When fire is used to provide light, leading a way,
Out of the darkness, providing warmth also.
Facing fire with faith also provides light and warmth.
Providing a path bathed in God's love.

WITNESS

Many times, two people are witness to the same event.
They often do not describe it in the same way.
We can have a similar day.
How we view it may depend on past content.

We are called to witness and give our testimony.
Not just in a court of law, but maybe in a ceremony.
A special day in church where we testify,
To what God has done in our life, as we verify.

Witness to the blessings God has provided.
Witness to His love and Grace.
Witness to who we are in Him.
Witness to the better person He makes us.

Sometimes it is hard to be a witness,
If we do though, one life may be changed.
We may not have to say anything to be a witness.
Our actions may demonstrate a life rearranged.

A FIRE WITHIN

A fire within, burning bright.
Brilliantly illuminating the night.
Feeling wonder at the sight,
Of the love we share, brought into the light.

A fire within, moving me to seek.
Soaring feelings, as if looking down from a high peak.
Taking away my power to speak.
Suddenly, facing the truth that I am weak.

A fire within, knowing that life is fleeting.
I need to see that I am meeting.
All the challenges that have been set.
By the One, sent by God, who I met.

A fire within, providing a direction.
Moving forward, under God's protection.
I strive to continue to thrive.
Feeling so very glad to be alive!

ACTIONS HAVE CONSEQUENCES

I often don't consider the consequences of my actions.
They only become apparent when I experience sanctions.
I am learning to give thought before I act.
An encouraging outcome is my increased tact.

The consequences I experience may vary in size,
Although some small actions may carry a big prize.
One small kindness may result in a big reward.
Especially, if the act is viewed and I get an award.

I can let that event to go to my head,
Thinking that I am as wonderful as everyone said.
Soon, another action may result in a different end.
Bringing all crashing down with much to mend.

I will attempt to act wisely in all I do.
Considering all the consequences too.
I do think I have found a better way.
If, before I act every time, I pray.

TRANSITIONS

Life is full of transitions, moving from one stage of life to the next.
Going from childhood to teenage years, leaving many parents vexed.
Entering young adulthood with many choices to make.
Deciding for the future and which path to take.

Transitions into full adulthood with responsibilities now
A career, job, dating with a view toward a marriage vow.
Making grown up choices on how to best live life
Dodging many disruptions that might lead to strife.

Transitions into marriage and parenthood, possibly
Learning a new role in life as a parent of a baby.
Feeling a bit unsure about this new role, maybe
Reading books, seeking guidance from others.

Transitions as our children grow from baby to toddler.
Time passes quickly as school days come and go.
Suddenly, older adulthood with experiences to know.
There are a few transitions left ahead, still time to grow.

RIGHTS AND
RESPONSIBILITIES

Rights may be demanded without a thought,
Of the responsibilities involved with those rights.
No longer wanting to think of naught and ought.
Part of those rights, obscuring how we got those rights.

Wanting to have all those rights,
Without participating in any of the fights.
That first won those rights,
Keeping all the rights within our sights.

Trying to protect our rights while ignoring.
The rights of others, over documents pouring,
To guarantee our rights and, possibly, taking away.
Rights that conflict with ours in any legal way.

It is everyone's responsibility to guarantee the rights,
Of all, not just a certain segment of the nation.
It should not matter what the station.
Held as equality exists only if all have the same rights.

DIRECTION #2

Each morning I arise, I pray.
What direction will I take today?
Is it my way or God's way?
What I decide will radically determine my day!

When the direction I take is my way.
It often leads me to a fragmented day.
Some things may turn out well.
Finding myself in a good place to dwell.

Often, my day goes downhill.
Reminding myself that God will always fulfill.
If I go His way, not mine
Everything will turn out fine.

Direction in life gives purpose and meaning.
Finding a goal into which I am leaning.
Without any direction, I may flounder.
Going through life is like a bounder.

DEPENDANCE

There are times when dependance is good.
Knowing that I need help, just elevating my mood.
If I ask for help, depending on others.
Remembering that asking for their help never bothers.

Dependance builds community,
As ability and gifts shared bring a unity.
Finding that I am not alone.
Can enable me to use my voice in a positive tone.

Dependance allows me to appreciate listening to another.
Realizing that I can grow and go further,
If I choose to depend, not do things my way.
Giving others a chance to have a say.

Dependance takes courage to admit a need.
No longer giving into pride as I proceed.
Creating a better future with God at the center.
A wonderful Christian life to enter.

FRAGMENTED

In life today, I see so much that is fragmented.
I find very little middle ground, no grey areas.
It is as if we have lost the art of compromise.
We see things from opposite spectrums.

Our schools, family, churches, and hospitals,
Have lost the ability to listen before speaking.
We can't seem to hear others or address issues.
We either want to have our way or bury our head.

Fragmented is a sad place to be.
I know it is not the way God wants it to be.
What can we do or say to find a better way?
Do we have to stay fragmented?

We let our views remain the same.
Not allowing any change
Dialog seems to be gone from our domain.
We speak but do listen to.

SPOKEN

I attempt to avoid bitter words spoken.
In anger, words are spoken.
Words that I can't take back.
I know it is self-control that I lack.

What I have spoken reflects what is in my heart.
I surprise myself with a start.
Suddenly aware of the anger that is a part,
Of my being, like a poisonous dart.

Awareness of my journey where I display,
Anger and frustration in the way.
My symptoms may come into play.
Adding many difficulties to my day.

My poems reflect things unspoken.
I can see, in black and white, what I have not spoken.
I can use my poems as a token.
A way to demonstrate I am not broken.

INSPIRING

I have found many people and places inspiring.
A life story depicting struggles one faces,
Or a song written from the heart that stirs.
A passion from the words serving as lures.

Watching a movie with a marvelous message to share.
Allowing the message to encourage me to show care.
Reading a book based on a remarkable true story.
Obstacles overcome to bring to God the glory.

Sometimes, God places an inspiring thought in my mind.
Starting a journey of exploration for me to find.
Ways to complete and fulfill the idea that was placed.
Continuing to see and feel as the idea is embraced.

What I find inspiring may not be so for you.
It may take some time to understand who,
Or what things are inspiring to you.
Recalling what God wants you to do.

PLACING MY LIFE
IN GOD'S HANDS

Every day is a new day.
I need to remember to choose His way,
Every day.
Letting His way hold sway.

Placing my life in God's hands,
Letting my life reveal where He stands.
Giving me His grace and love.
Unconditional love that is His alone.

As I place my life in His hands, He leads me.
He is there with me in everything, so I can see.
He is in control, giving me strength when needed.
His words provide necessary guidance indeed.

Placing my life in God's hands, moment by moment,
Not allowing any doubt or rebellion to foment.
Knowing that He will never forsake me.
He will shape me into who I am to be.

IN GOD'S TIMING

It has taken me many years to consider the timing,
Of events will never be my timing, it is God's timing.
That matters in everything we do in life always,
It will fail until we listen to what and when He says.

In God's timing, what we do will make a difference.
If what we do does succeed, we can make the inference,
That it is being done at the time He has chosen.
All other times, our actions may be frozen.

There are many unknowns we encounter daily.
God knows what we do not; He deals fairly.
Guiding us in our actions if we let Him.
He does nothing on a whim.

In God's timing and His plan, great things occur.
Sometimes happening so fast, it seems a blur.
We can trust in God's timing as we must.
For, if we don't, our life will be a bust.

OUTLOOK

Do we view events in a positive or negative way?
How do we interpret what others say?
Is our glass half empty or half full?
Do we feel it necessary to fill a conversational lull?

Our outlook on life determines the actions we take.
If we see things positively, our feelings won't break.
When someone challenges our view,
We fail to act on a negative cue.

If we see our glass as half empty, we may be a pessimist.
If we see our glass half full, we may be an optimist.
The pessimist tends to anticipate the bad.
Leaving much of life is viewed as sad.

Our outlook may cause us to fill every lull.
Not feeling comfortable with silence, feeling a pull,
To fill each moment of silence with any sound.
Even if no one at all is around!

STEADFAST

I hope that I am steadfast in my faith every day,
As it means I hold tightly in an unwavering way.
To my beliefs and my action matches my words,
I don't back away from trials, but I move towards.

If I am steadfast, I know God is always with me.
In any trials, it is in His hands I will be.
I address God and listen as I live each day,
And choose to trust Him and obey.

Steadfast in my faith gives me courage to speak out.
Taking the words God gives me, sometimes to shout.
What His words offer me as I travel on my way.
As with my words, I continue to act after I pray.

Steadfast gives me grace as I know at times.
Acting alone, my actions will go down in flames.
God will pick me up and forgive if I repent.
Reminding me again of the time with Him I've spent.

HEALING

Psalm 23:4 "Even when I go through the darkest valley, I fear no danger, for you are with me, your rod and your staff- they comfort me."

TRAVELING ON

I tend to stay on a certain path as I travel from here to there.
But occasionally, I may stop and ask do I care?
Whether that is the place I want to be.
Does it give a purpose and a choice for me,
Or is it just a stop along the way to rest?
Contemplating all my choices, consider what is best.
As I am traveling on, I try to think outside the box,
And look at many paths, taking one that unlocks.
All the creative ways to live my life today,
As I travel on along my way.

WORDS

There is an abundance of words sometimes.
How they are used can often be viewed as crimes.
Words can be used to help someone heal,
Or they can be allowed to conceal.
Words themselves have no meaning.
As they are spoken, words reveal where we are leaning.
Words can be used in good ways,
Leading to productive days,
Or words can cause us to be sad.
Especially, if the words used are bad.
We must remember the words we use,
Can shape our identity and, maybe, confuse.
How others see us and how we relate to each other.
Whether we are seen as good for one another,
Or if we are seen as a huge bother.

WHAT IF

The world was a happy safe place.
For all of us living in this space.
If no one had to wonder,
Or stave off hunger.
Because every person would have.
No one would be a slave,
To their emotions.
Understanding the notion,
That all are made.
Created, with all our parts laid,
Out by one great power.
One who will tower,
Overall living things.
And all man brings,
To allow God some mirth,
From all happenings here on earth.

CELEBRATION

I like to think of life as a celebration.
Finding wonder on each occasion.
Knowing I feel joy in each day,
If I think and act in this way.
No longer can the negative thoughts hold sway.
I can allow them to go away.
Even the word celebration has a positive spin.
Keeping myself well, not letting my illness win.
Depression and anxiety held at bay,
As I accept and live with bipolar, feeling okay.
Celebration holds the key.
Now I can truly see.

MANIA

Everything was spinning, out of control.
Lack of sleep is taking its toll.
Mind is racing, unable to keep facing,
Thoughts are so fast, can't keep focus.
Knowing my illness is the locus.
Determining mania is now full blown.
Understanding that triggers should be known.
I can control the situation before,
Mania symptoms come to the fore.
Moving so fast, feeling invincible.
Failing to acknowledge the principle.
I can change what I do, you can too.
Mania can sneak up on you.
Sometimes we allow our symptoms to woo.
We like that energy and feeling like a superhero,
But neglecting to remember what happened next.
Often, at the crash, we feel vexed.

MENTAL HEALTH

Circumstances have increased the focus on mental health.
Acknowledging the decreasing amount of wealth.
Resulting from the costs of not facing.
The needs of mental illness far outpacing.
Resources available and the costs to develop.
Programs necessary so symptoms no longer envelop.
Keeping the potential for future generations,
At a lower level, because we have failed.
To make mental health a priority, instead we have railed,
Social issues directly impacted by lack of mental health.
Allowing our own inaction to increase its' silent stealth.
Until we recognize the enormous loss,
If we do not choose to place increasing focus,
On the importance of our mental health.

CALMING SEA

It is amazing when I gaze at the sea.
The calming effects it has on me.
The beautiful reflection of the sun,
As it grazes across the water in one,
Swoop as it makes it run.
Highlighting the colors in its' wake.
Allowing all the anxiety and stress to forsake.
So, I can enjoy the calming effects to take.
Meditating on the wonders of the sea.
The calmness it grants to me.

MUSIC FOR MY SOUL

Listening in as the bow traveled slowly across the strings of the violin.
I would hear the notes blend into a mournful tune.
As the bow traveled more swiftly now,
The mournful tune became livelier.
Not quite a jig yet, but on its' way.
Feet tapping faster with the music holding sway.
This is the music for my soul.
Wishing that making music was my goal.
Knowing that learning to play becomes harder every day.
So, I will just sit and enjoy,
All the music for my soul, with joy.
I listen as each tune serves to buoy.
Feelings I thought would never be destroyed.
The desire for music to feed my soul.

HOME

The cruise was one of the best,
And I did manage to get some needed rest.
Now I am home with much to do.
Trying to find balance in rest and activity too.

Home is the place that I find most safe.
Knowing well the people and places,
The routine of my days and unexpected surprises.
Make my life relatively free from strife.

Although I enjoyed the places I saw, I am glad,
To be home to resume my new normal.
A little less anxious as I encountered.
A peace and acceptance of the current situation.

I was again reminded of the unity.
That exists in another country.
Where, although, we have differences.
We all have God's assurances.

Home is a place in my heart.
It has been with my husband from the start.
We have traveled the world for many years.
We have overcome many fears.

Home is now here with children.
Scattered, but I have one grown child here.
I enjoy seeing others, not often enough.
Not seeing grandchildren can be tough.

Home is still the place with my husband by my side.
I wouldn't change much, just wish mountains were present.
I really can't resent where I now reside.
My husband beside me, I am fully alive.

AN END TO VIOLENCE

An end to violence is my prayer.
I know it can be done, but only if we act as one.
We must teach love, not hate before it is too late.

An end to violence in our schools.
Providing our teachers with the tools.
Everyone is laying down blame and shame.

An end to violence in our streets.
Offering more positive actions, rather than sanctions,
To those in gangs as better options.

An end to violence against our nurses.
Not taking out our frustrations about our situations.
Nurses are only there because they care.

An end to violence in our lives.
As together we strive to see beyond our differences,
Coming together as children of God.

SHADES OF GRAY

We view issues as black or white,
That view is not always right.
There are many shades of gray.
We fail to see to have our way.

Shades of gray let us see,
In a different way what can be.
A compromise of sorts to allow,
A new path to follow.

When we see shades of gray,
We can bend to take a different way.
Not always having to be right,
And maybe exercise our might.

Shades of gray can enable us.
To accept things without fuss.
We can walk a middle path.
No longer having to react with wrath.

CANCER OF THE SOUL

A cancer of the soul exists every time a person resists,
A change in how we treat each with our behavior.
Indicating a definite lack of knowing our Savior,
We treat each other with disdain, showing us as very vain.

It is the unkindness we see on social media.
As we spew venom in the posts we make,
Never imagine the harm and pain.
We inflict because we show no restrain.

Cancer exists because we show no remorse.
As we continue to chart a course,
Where anger, distrust, and disrespect are present.
No longer acting with love or seeking any consent.

A cancer of the soul exists in how we spend our time.
There is a disconnect as we fail to intervene seeing a crime.
We watch violence and crime on TV but fail to see.
The real-life effect it has on you and me

SIGH OF RELIEF

There are certain expressions I often hear.
A sigh of relief is one.
Often said after we have nothing more to fear,
Or when everything we had to do is done.

I think the sound is slightly different in tone.
From the sigh of disappointment often heard.
When something is not done,
Or the occurrence of something you feared.

My children say from time to time.
They can tell when I give a sigh.
Even when the context is unclear, at times.
They complain that my expectations are too high.

I am unaware of those sighs I express.
Just as I am unaware of humming.
I don't think I could suppress it.
Things of which I am unaware, so I cease trying.

BOUNDARIES

I used to have no boundaries,
Which left me in quandaries.
As no limits, was I making,
So, everyone kept taking.

Now, I have boundaries on my time.
All the people in my life try to make it a crime.
I find myself very relieved.
Owing to these boundaries I've conceived.

Boundaries are necessary for my mental health.
Preventing my symptoms, coming in stealth.
It assists me so my bipolar journey is good.
I was able to take the measures I could.

It has taken me too long,
To do this because I wanted to belong.
I realized a few years too late,
To not belong is a better fate.

*COMFORT

When I think of comfort, I think of spending time at ease.
Reading in a reclining chair with a fan providing a breeze,
Or relaxing in a mountain cabin with a beautiful view,
Not having to do anything nor pay attention to a cue.

Comfort may be giving strength to someone
To ease the loss of a friend or loved one.
Or the sense of relief when you overcome,
Not having to deal with any bad things to come.

Do I seek comfort above all else?
How does my comfort affect others?
If I stay in my comfort zone, what do I miss?
I may miss a lot in my Christian life.

If I live in comfort, do I see the discomfort of others?
If I live in comfort, do I show care?
If I live in comfort, I may never dare?
Dare to venture out and share my faith!

RESTORATION

Restoration is a hard concept to grasp.
Done well, it will cause you to gasp.
Time and perseverance can get it right.
The results will offer a beautiful sight.

Restoration of a relationship is not an easy task.
Sometimes achieved, often we choose to don a mask,
Hiding our feelings, our attempts at repair to stop.
Lacking complete restoration, the relationship will drop.

Restoration of a feeling is hard to bring back.
Never fully realizing what we may lack
We took a certain path that brought rewards.
A restoration of that path may be a way to move forwards.

A terrible storm may destroy our dwelling or house.
Seeking restoration from the storm may arouse
Anxious moments from the storm's torments.
Seeking reasons for restorations' lack, we try another tack.

IMPATIENCE AND IRRITATION

Two traits I have found go together in my bipolar journey,
Impatience and irritation increase if I lose sight on my journey.
I hurry people and projects along with little patience shown.
I snap and demonstrate a lack of control, for which I am known.

If I am paying attention, I realize I am in trouble.
I need to make changes before my troubles double.
It took me some time to recognize these traits.
Now I do, which warns me of what awaits.

It helps me on my journey to be aware.
I won't have to suddenly stare
Into a bleak future with uncontrolled moods.
I can navigate the deep woods.

I strive for patience and self-control.
Needing help to develop these traits,
My impatience and irritation won't take a toll.
Learning the difference when one waits.

SOUL MATE

One of the most fortunate events in my life to this day
Is meeting my soul mate as God found a way
To move me towards His plans for the direction I would go.
Forever changing my life, on a path so different from before.

I am blessed for having my soul mate
With me for forty-eight years, not by fate.
It was never in my plans to lead a military life,
I was a civilian nurse who hoped someday to be a wife.

I left my comfort zone to join the Air Force,
An unknown way of life to me, on a new course.
I traveled to several states I had never seen,
Going places, I had never been.

I did not meet my soul mate right away.
God used many zig-zag paths to lead the way
To the right time and place to meet
The soul mate I daily greet.

WELLNESS

I don't think wellness is just the absence of disease.
It can be a balance in my life between work and ease.
If I work or play all the time, I will be unbalanced,
Everything would be serious or fun with one side silenced.

Wellness is a balance with health on a continuum,
Mental, physical, and spiritual wellness as a sum
Of everything I do to balance my life each day.
Using so many resources to find my way.

My wellness is determined by how I live.
If I do things in excess, my balance will give.
If I don't do enough exercise or eat enough food
I may find myself not feeling very good.

Wellness is a choice I make through each day.
When I succeed in that balance, my health I display.
Everything in moderation is the motto for me,
Providing every day, my wellness to see.

COMMUNITY OF BELIEVERS

I am blessed to be a member of a community of believers.
Bathed in God's love, I am one of the receivers
Of God's grace, already so strong
In faith due to this group to which I belong.

It is in this community that I am fed.
Bringing me to this spiritual journey where I am led.
I hear the Word of God, but it is in action
My growth in faith gets its' traction.

A community of believers may be composed
Of many diverse members who are supposed
To blend these differences to act as a community.
Acting together in faith to show unity.

God uses this community of believers greatly.
If we remember to give our all completely,
Working together to spread His Word,
Knowing His Word is stronger than any sword.

SILENCE THE VIOLENCE

We need a voice of reason to silence the violence.
A quiet, self-assured voice overcoming the noise.
The shouting to be heard while no-one listens.
Someone with no agenda, other than to show love.

If we fail to silence the violence, very little will change.
Violence will continue, getting to be the way
Any disagreement will be settled.
There will be no winner in the fray.

Silence the violence as we find an answer.
That takes away the anger we display.
Being quick to listen, slow to speak and anger
Is a quote from James 1:19 in the Bible.

There is always a better way than violence.
The Prince of Peace has shown the way.
Loving God and each other will help save the day.
Bringing silence to the violence as we pray.

ENVY

I find that envy can creep up on me, if I am not careful.
In those times I compare myself to others, I need to get an earful
Of verses in the Bible that speak to me of envy,
The consequences when I don't see what envy does to me.

It causes me to covet what is not mine to have.
I have the life, gifts, and opportunities God gave.
If I have envy, I am not grateful, but sinful,
In my relationship to God, I've lost something beautiful.

Envy causes separation in many relationships, not just with God.
I find myself in isolation from friends as to that envy, I gave a nod.
I can turn inward and fail to seek the Lord,
Finding myself alone from Christian friends, cutting the cord.

I surround myself with fellowship and the Word.
I remember what the Bible says of envy, causing discord.
If I find myself starting to compare what I do with another
I understand that I am the only one it will bother.

INVIGORATED

When I find my energy flagging
And as a result, my body is dragging.
I find I need to be invigorated.
By the one in whose image, I am created.

Many times, I am stopped in my tracks
Because I fail to rest and relax to avoid the cracks.
I find in my whole being because I am not seeing,
Too tired to view the wonder as inside I am trying.

In His words and presence, I am invigorated.
By His living water, I am fully sated.
Through my prayers and fellowship, my cup is full.
All my doubts and questions answered, I am whole.

I stand with a purpose as I am invigorated in His word.
He sends me on a mission in this life to go forward,
Telling of my journey, from beginning to the end.
How I hope to have an eternity with Him to spend.

HERE AND NOW

It is hard to stay in the here and now.
We want to move forward or look back to show
How far we have come or what we have done,
The things in our life that have been hard won.

Here and now allows us to be free
To let go of the past or what we want to be.
We can simply enjoy who we are now
Living life fully in every way we know how.

In the here and now, we let go of any regret,
No longer seeing anything to cause us to fret.
We don't have to plan for a tomorrow,
Each day comes with both joy and sorrow.

We aren't promised tomorrow so live for today.
Here and now thinking is the way
To answer the challenge of staying okay,
Not letting anxiety about our life have any say.

A LOVING TRUTH

Deception can start with a small lie that grows.
A story I remember well is Pinocchio,
Who had a nose which always grows
On every occasion where he told a lie.

A truth can be told in many ways.
It can be told in a straightforward manner
With little concern with how it is received.
The truth can hurt.

The truth can be told in the form of a story,
Given in a roundabout manner
With loving concern for the one intended
To hear the truth so the hurt is less.

We all need to hear the truth, so we are guided.
The way the truth is relayed.
Does make a difference in how it is received.
Given in love, it is received in love.

FAITHFUL

If I were asked to define faithful, I would reflect on Lucky,
A barely weaned puppy found in a recycling bin.
Sick with heartworms, not sure he would live.
Many transfusions later under a vet's care, he survived.

He was a gentle giant who followed me around.
Although my daughter found him, I was his person.
He was faithful when I was in a deep depression,
Staying by my side, seeming to know how I was feeling.

At the age of six, even under meds, he had heartworms.
He survived the months of treatment, becoming an indoor dog.
At the age of twelve, he went out back.
He would not come in again.

We found a wonderful vet who lovingly cared.
He died at home surrounded by his faithful family.
He no longer suffered, but oh how we miss Lucky
As we remember, he was faithful to the end.

GIVING MYSELF PERMISSION

I have found I let many events from my past hold me back.
Seeming to see only the things that I lack.
Giving myself permission to let go and move on
Allows me to see more clearly, all obstacles gone.

Giving myself permission to let go of the judgements made
By others and I so I can continue on this path, not delayed,
No longer looking to be a people pleaser,
Letting God give me strength and be a tension releaser.

Giving myself permission to rest in His arms,
Not giving into Satan's charms.
Fully seeing who God wants me to become,
As I allow His Word into my heart to come.

Giving myself permission to let go of any worry,
As I go forward, repenting my actions and saying I am sorry.
Knowing that God has forgiven me,
I must forgive myself and just be.

HEALING FROM WITHIN

Healing from within takes time and effort.
If we have a wound that just heals on the outside,
We may think that all is well and experience comfort.
But the wound is still buried on the inside.

We may take steps to heal relationships,
Doing everything in a superficial way,
Not digging deeply into what chips
At the relationship, allowing the relationship to fray.

Healing our nation from within will take
Enormous strength of will so we can make
Decisions that are not based on emotion
Or selfish desires for power that are put into motion.

Healing from within doesn't mean a band-aid
Applied to a gash will allow any healing or closure.
The gap between the skin will not fade,
Or heal our great divide, of that, I am sure.

DIGNITY

I have witnessed people who possess a great deal of dignity.
The characteristics are hard to describe but I feel that integrity
Is a major player as well as outward appearance and style
To respect and care for self as they take care of others for a while.

I feel that care givers show great dignity in their concern.
They go over and above any reward they earn.
The best care givers understand they need time
Caring for themselves to continue to stay in their prime.

Dignity in carriage and action and words describe
A few people I know who give off a vibe
That shouts of dignity to which they ascribe
As everything they are and do seem to jibe.

Dignity develops over time, I think,
Given opportunities that bring them to the brink,
Offering them the tools to show
A dignity and character they are privileged to know.

CHOOSING TO BE
VULNERABLE AND REAL

As a child of God, I know He loves me no matter what,
Regardless of who I am or who I am not,
Revealing the real me to others, leaving myself vulnerable,
Letting me show a God who is able.

A God who can lift me up and show me love,
I can show others the real me and stand above
The events and things that could tear me down,
God provides joy and a smile, not sorrow and a frown.

A God who I share with others as much as I can,
A Christian who shows love and compassion to fellow man,
Not wearing a mask to keep others at bay,
Always choosing to follow Jesus as the Way.

Choosing to be vulnerable and real,
Allowing God to rule my head and my heart,
Serving others with passion and zeal,
Content as God is my focus from the start.

CONTINUUM

Viewing all things as being on a continuum can be
Eye opening, as it addresses a change we can see.
At birth, we need care and touch from our mother.
At death, we need care and touch by another.

If we look at our health as traveling
On a continuum from one level to another,
We may be less likely to be unraveling,
Letting worry and fear be a bother.

There may be years when we seem stable.
Our continuum showing us to be able
To maintain an unvarying balance,
Showing no change in status, little dalliance.

Continuum can be useful in providing hope,
Giving us mechanisms so we can cope.
Allowing us to see clearly where we are,
Knowing, on this continuum, we can go far.

A HEALING FAITH

There have been times in my life when faith has saved me.
How difficult my journey with mental illness would be,
Without my trust and belief in God, a foundation for
Faith, and all those experiences which form the core
Of who I am and what my life will be. With faith at the center,
Allowing the influence of God in my life to enter,
Faith may grow or faith may die.
It all depends on who or what we rely.
If faith in God is our focus, not some hocus-pocus,
To bring us through a difficult time
It would be such a crime.
With no person or place to turn,
No way in which to learn,
The value of life is founded on faith.

INQUIRING

Deuteronomy 4:29 "But from there, you will search for the Lord your God, and you will find him with all your heart and all your soul."

GETTING READY TO LAND

The ship continues on its' voyage, almost done
As more land appears on the horizon.
The growing realization of a dream
Is somehow more exciting than it would seem.

There are many more signs of land.
It's almost as if I could reach out my hand.
And touch the visions of sand
Now appearing before my eyes
As the land separates from the skies.

We are much closer now,
Wondering when and how
I will act to see some sights
I haven't seen it in many years of days and nights.

Continuing on through the fjords
As memories increase as I move towards
The land I will never forget.
My mind continues to call up pictures of the past,
Getting me ready to land at last.

WANTING A RESET

As my journey nears its' finish
I find myself making a wish
I could have a reset to start again,
Wanting to find myself about to begin.

Over half the journey is in the past
Wishing I could make the remaining time last.
All I want is a reset,
Even though all my dreams have been met.

Wanting a reset, although not possible
Is so understandable,
Since I have enjoyed myself through and through
Recognizing this reset fantasy can't come true.

ECHOES

Echoes in my mind of past events,
Hoping to use them, some wisdom to find.
Knowing that the past events can help me grow,
Learning from the results of my actions to know.

Echoes of what happened are lessons to be learned.
Definitely not anything to be spurned.
If I heed these echoes, not choosing to forget,
I can change my future, making it better yet.

Echoes of the past can hold me fast,
Either serving to make a new tomorrow
Or repeating my mistakes, leading me to sorrow.
Only I can choose what echoes I keep or lose.

Echoes through history do prove
We do not always make a move
To change the events of the past,
Making some bad decisions last.

EXCUSES

Excuses are a tiring thing to hear.
As someone chooses to say "I can't because …"
Offering up a lame reason as the cause
For whatever isn't happening as time draws near.

Excuses may be used as a way
To not be held accountable,
For their lack of actions or not doing what they say,
Not putting forth any effort, even if they are able.

Excuses may have some validity,
If the actions of someone else, prevent their ability
To do what is asked or promised,
Causing a delay or opportunity that is missed.

Excuses are rarely pleasing
To the one who hears them said,
Many times, wishing those excuses would be ceasing.
The many excuses that cause them to see red.

LIMITATIONS

At times, I find it hard to see my limitations,
To realize I need to ask for help in certain situations.
I find it daunting to see and recognize what I lack.
I want to be able to reach a goal and stay on track.

The times I sit back and really see what I can and cannot do,
To truly understand what my limitations are and know who
I can turn to and allow God to lead me by the hand,
Letting me know that He will always understand.

Limitations can hold you back and see things in a negative way.
Or you can use them to lead you to have a better day,
Allowing other people to provide help to overcome
Your limitations as a unity of purpose will come.

It is true that everyone has limitations of some sort.
And I am very happy to report,
My limitations have served me well,
As I work with others, not letting my limitations to dwell.

REFLECTIVE

We can be reflective about our past.
We can't change it or what was cast.
Being reflective, we can recognize
As wisdom gained from steps taken to realize.

If we are not reflective, we may miss
Changes, good and bad, that now exist.
People and opportunities God placed before us,
He used to shape our life, despite the fuss.

At the time, we failed to see
What God allowed us simply to be.
Present in every day as we found our way,
Being content in who we are today.

Reflective so we can shine a light
On the need to depend on God's might.
Knowing, in this life, we are never alone,
We have God's presence and His gifts to hone.

REPERCUSSIONS

Failing to foresee the repercussions that will be
When we act without thinking, never blinking,
Or seeking guidance on the best way to go,
Acting on impulse and causing such woe.

Repercussions can trigger a cascade
Of events that are so big we can't wade
Through to get to a better place,
Never finding a safe space.

Always be ready to face repercussions,
As acting without thinking never cushions
The results of our actions, so we need to learn
How to proceed to prevent any bridges to burn.

It is hard to undo what has been done.
Focusing on repercussions can lead one
To see and understand that the actions we take
Can be better if informed decisions we make.

NOTIONS ABOUT DEVOTIONS

I hold certain notions about devotions,
Seeing them as important but not essential.
In the past two years, this shifted in a way substantial,
I have to start each day, living in The Way.

When I start each day reading The Bible
I know that in everything I do is liable
To reflect the type of Christian life I display,
I want to honor God by demonstrating His Way.

I find myself reading slowly, meditating on His Word
Knowing that nothing I do here will enable me to afford
What I have freely been given by God's Grace.
No action by me can a relationship with Him replace.

My notions about devotions show a growth I can see,
Becoming a better Christian and a better me.
I give to God the glory every time I share my story.
I know that every day He carries me along my way.

*SEEKING HIS KINGDOM FIRST

Sometimes, in seeking His Kingdom first, I derail.
As attempting to accomplish something in my own strength, I fail.
I know my weakness reveals His strength.
His power expands always in its' breadth and length.

Seeking His Kingdom first paves the path I am on
When all the cares close in, in His power, they are gone.
Every day, the prayers and devotions show me the way.
All His plans for my life are at play.

Knowing God is in control, even when many don't think so.
Gives me the incentive to continue to grow.
As I seek His Kingdom first, feeling comfort in His grace.
I can see a little bit of Heaven in this place.

The peace and joy I feel today.
Even in trials and troubles, I am okay.
Because I sought His Kingdom first
His power and love filled me until I almost burst.

SHALLOW VERSUS DEEP

When it comes to water, I prefer to be in the shallow end.
When it comes to my thoughts, I hope I dwell in the deep end.
As I look at things on the surface, I may be wrong.
Judging and going with the throng

It is easier at times to stay amid the shallow.
Never going deeper or seeking to follow
A path leading to a deeper understanding.
And possibly a more suitable ending

If my life journey is a shallow one, I will never.
See the truth leading me to the One who is forever!
Always with me throughout my days
Demonstrating His deeper ways

I will choose to dwell in the deep
Seeking God even when I sleep
He gives me words to write.
Often in the middle of the night

BEGINNING AND END

We all have a beginning and an end.
Paths vary as some are straight, others bend.
Following a straight and narrow path can be very hard.
If we follow our path alone, we are constantly on guard.

I have found that each bend in the road.
Can be a challenge if I do it on my own.
Sometimes, I need another voice to goad.
I can turn to God or a voice over the phone.

I haven't always turned to God but instead.
I listened to another as my anticipation turned to dread.
As I age, I see a pattern forming in my head.
If I listen to God, my life will always be ahead.

At the end, I will see God's hand in all I did.
Even when I didn't follow what He said.
He met me at each bend and waited.
Always with me as my troubles abated.

DECIPHERING DREAMS

Many times, I have a dream that stays with me into the day.
I understand that those dreams show me God's way.
If I try to decipher them on my own, I fail.
When the Holy Spirit is present, those dreams set sail.

A life without dreams is hard to imagine, very dull.
It is the dreams we hold in our heart, making it full.
That makes life an interesting adventure and will.
Sustain us through the times when we are still!

I dream in color with vivid pictures that may seem strange.
Deciphering them can be a challenge as I arrange.
The sequence of the dream where events may seem.
In great disorder, not sure sometimes that it is a dream.

If I awake without a distinct memory of the dream
I am sure that God's presence was not in the dream.
I have more confidence in deciphering dreams today.
As I spend more time with God every day

PROMISE TO KEEP

Making promises impossible to keep often makes me weep.
All the good intentions of keeping the promise may sweep.
Away any underlying concerns about my ability to keep.
That promise as I find myself in an abyss so deep.

A promise made and not kept can hurt.
My word given will be treated as dirt.
No longer will anything I say be believed.
A future promise will not be received.

Promises are important to establish.
What I say I will do and not just a wish
An offer was made in a moment with no follow through.
An empty promise, showing a lack of integrity to you.

Promises made must be thoroughly considered.
Can the promise be kept or delivered?
As made or will it be broken, not showing a token
Of esteem to the one to whom the promise was made

STUBBORNNESS OR DETERMINATION

We think stubbornness is an unwillingness to change.
Decisions we make or actions we take, so strange.
Others see stubbornness more as determination.
In the face of obstacles as we overcome the situation

Stubbornness is seen as a negative trait.
Determination is viewed as a positive state.
Where perseverance allows us to stay a course
Having a goal in mind, willing to utilize any source.

I think there is a definite difference between the two.
Stubbornness may cause you to stagnant with the same view.
Determination moves you forward to claim the prize.
Doing new things, accomplishing more than you surmise

I try not to confuse the two and let determination rule.
Being stubborn about some things can sometimes fuel.
Discontent and disharmony in how I live.
Maybe, keeping me at a loss with nothing to give

CREATION

The moon, sun, stars, and planets exist.
Humans, other mammals, birds, fish and other species exist.
Moments, hours, days pass as day turns into night, years pass.
Creation covers all that exists and will always encompass.

As we grow, some questions about creation arise.
Many mysteries to solve, wanting answers to be concise.
Knowing that we will be disappointed to find.
Some answers will never enter our mind.

Creation is viewed with awe and wonder.
Providing many thoughts to ponder
Our relationship to the Earth, the people and animals within
Not understanding what actions will cause us to lose or win.

Creation continues with changes, both good and bad
Often, we miss what we once had.
Trying to go back to an earlier time.
Ignoring the problems of that earlier time

THE CALLING

I believe we each have a calling, but we must choose.
We must believe in order to pursue, or we lose.
The chance to see where that calling will lead.
To realize that we have the fortitude to succeed.

My calling, I believe, came to me when I was young.
It may have developed from the people I was among
I was surrounded by medical personnel but drawn.
To the nurses as the wish to become a nurse did dawn

The pursuit of the calling did not come easy.
The years of study were in no way breezy.
The courses of study required much work.
And many difficulties to succeed in my calling did lurk.

The realization of that calling left no regrets.
The experiences in that calling were as good as it gets.
If I had ignored that call, I would not have seen.
The people and traveled to the places that I have been.

BUILDING A RELATIONSHIP

There are steps you need to take in building a relationship.
It cannot be one sided with one person in the lead.
Respect and communication are necessary to equip.
Each person in the relationship for it to succeed.

Building a relationship requires time and commitment.
Both parties invested to see it through
As each person recognizes a balance with no resentment
For the relationship provides a support to accrue

Building a relationship provides a framework.
To develop solutions to problems as we work
Together with a single goal to successfully plan.
The steps to be taken and do everything we can.

It isn't easy to do anything if a relationship fails.
No solid foundation has been formed and everyone bails.
Time and commitment were not there.
It was impossible for those in the relationship to share.

STEPPINGSTONES

When I look back, I see many steppingstones.
Leading me to where I am today with overtones,
Of where I started from, moving forward until,
I reach a point where all my goals, I fulfill.

Those steppingstones are full of failure too.
I learn so much more from failure than I do,
From all the success that I later knew.
The mistakes I made were more than a few.

Steppingstones can be difficult to see at the time.
A plan may not survive as it is not the right time.
New steppingstones are needed, old ideas weeded.
Starting afresh to make a new plan that will succeed.

Steppingstones to make a path to reach a place,
Taking our time and not seeking to race.
Enjoying our way at a deliberate pace.
Able to meet and overcome any obstacles we face.

A DIVIDING LINE

My life has a dividing line.
Pre diagnosis, I seemed just fine.
Post diagnosis, my life took a dive.
With care, I managed to stay alive.

The dividing line went from being whole.
To a journey which would take a toll
Feeling different in many ways
On a roller coaster for quite a few days

Today, there are more years spent.
Appearing whole, no reason to vent
No longer sure which is the better half of the line.
As the second part brought me closer to the divine

The dividing line marked the beginning of stronger belief.
Feeling myself closer to a God who provided relief.
Knowing that I am held in his hands every day.
Gives me hope that I am finding a better way.

INSIGHT

Often, I seek to find more understanding and insight.
It is only in my morning devotions and prayers that I see light.
God gives me answers in each devotion that I read.
He offers me more insight than I will ever need.

Insight can help me find solutions when I see none.
I can seek the answer from a greater one.
If I start each day with God, I am never alone.
It is the insight I receive from Him that sets the tone.

Insight provides depth to my belief.
Knowing that God provides gives me relief.
Trusting that God is always there.
Encourages that insight to freely share.

Insight to follow God's plan, no matter how hard.
Following His way and letting down my guard
God provides others to help me along my way.
With the Holy Spirit giving me the words to say

DIVING DEEP

There are certain thoughts God brings into my mind.
It is in the poems that I write that you can find.
Me diving deep to look beyond the surface.
Often finding something God wants me to face.

Diving deep has helped me so I overcome
Not letting my diagnosis define who I become.
Lately three words have been my focus.
Depression, oppression, and suppression; my locus

Putting down myself, others, and my ideas
Measuring myself against others, unable to cease
Unaware of what I am doing or why.
Until I turn to God, who always helps me get by

Awareness of what I am doing settles in
Knowing that God's love will win.
Helps me embrace myself and others to see.
We are all God's children, including me.

FULL OR EMPTY?

My lack of energy can be a sign of a certain state of mind.
Recognizing the importance of awareness to find
Is my energy level a result of too much to do?
Or the depression part of my illness starting to brew.

Bipolar symptoms can shape my life, if I am unaware.
Trying to keep everything inside and not share.
All that I am feeling because I am scared.
Afraid of deep depression and not prepared.

If I am feeling too full of life, am I soaring.
Into mania and unable to keep from pouring
I jump into too many activities, getting no sleep.
Too wired up to follow the routines I normally keep.

Because I have Bipolar, I can never be sure.
Is my energy level due to the mental illness with no cure?
Or a physical problem that can be resolved
I must be aware of all that is involved.

DISCERNMENT

Many times, I struggle for discernment to be given.
I know I am not alone in this, but I feel driven.
To understand and follow God's plan for me.
I will never be sure, but I must trust and see.

Discernment is a gift from the one above.
Given by the God who shows love.
One thought makes a loop through my mind.
It'll be given to me at the time I am to seek and find.

Discernment only comes as I am in tune with God.
When I stray, an unexpected occurrence may prod.
Me back to see that my walk must match my talk.
If they don't, how can new disciples not fail to balk?

Discernment allows me to see, only briefly.
A certain passage of the Bible that deals chiefly.
With an experience or decision, I must make
God will open my eyes to what is at stake.

TIMELESS

On occasion, I heard someone remark.
That a person or event was timeless
A remark that left me in the dark
For quite a while, I do confess.

Now, I think that time does not define.
The person or event concerned.
It is not just used as a line.
There is a meaning, I have learned.

When something is timeless,
There is no date or age to identify.
The relevance is limitless.
Nothing outdated to spy.

Timeless is always current in style.
Never giving away any evidence
Of how much time has passed while
Sometimes it may be centuries, I sense.

JUSTICE

Esther 4:14 "If you keep silent at this time, relief and deliverance will come to the Jewish people from another place, but you and your father's family will be destroyed. Who knows, perhaps, you have come to your royal position for such a time as this."

MOTHER EARTH

The planet that we live on, we call her Mother Earth
But we don't always respect her as we should at our birth.
We are taught to honor our parents.
Not taught to honor Mother Earth as she warrants
We pollute the air and are not fair.
We toss our trash without a thought.
Not thinking of all she has brought.
The sights and sounds of nature.
Comfort she brings to each creature.
What would we do without the song of birds?
No view of wondrous animals in herds
No smell of different flowers
No sign of the sun or moon as it lowers.
We need to think about our choices.
Do we want to silence Mother Earth's voices?

RACISM

It is often I have a heavy heart.
We observe outward appearance and start.
To make assumptions based on color
I include myself, if I were fined a dollar.
For every time I made a wrong assumption
A hefty fine would be mine, so God give me the gumption.
To freely admit that I do see color, but I pray to look.
Beyond to see all the wrong turns my assumptions took
No longer hold to be true for me.
It is a child of God that I now see.

MAKING A DIFFERENCE

Sometimes, we fail to see that our small actions can make.
A difference, not just in us, in the path we and others take.
It may be a small gesture of kindness in a line.
Starting a domino effect is hard to define.

Making a difference can start in our family.
Shown in our openness to others and hospitality.
When we make ourselves available to another
Regardless of what the world may see as a bother.

A hand up offered with no strings attached, given in love.
Reflecting the lessons Jesus taught, His love from above.
Listening without judgement in a conversation
Really hearing what is said leaves a good sensation.

Making a difference can be just a smile and a greeting
Leaving the person receiving an acknowledgement of meeting
Someone who finds value in them, making their day brighter.
And lessening any heavy load they may carry, feeling lighter.

*DELIVERANCE

I need deliverance when I see myself as the center.
Not putting others first or asking God to enter
Wrapped up in what I need, not planting any seeds.
To take hold and increase my faith, just growing weeds.

Deliverance from viewing things as the world does
Not seeing the One who can take my woes.
Providing strength to meet the challenges today.
My deliverance will come in His way.

Deliverance from the wrong things I have done.
As I repent and am forgiven by the One
No matter what I may do, God offers love,
Forgiveness, and deliverance to me from above

RESTORE ME AGAIN

Facing a loss, it becomes important to seek restoration.
I am asking God to restore me again with my cooperation.
Often, I ask but do not wait for an answer from God.
Cooperation means following His lead (and nod)

So much has happened this week as I long.
To be restored, letting go of the bad and sad.
I seek to dwell on the good and remember.
To thank God for each family member

I need God to restore me again so I can be.
An able partner for my husband and we
Can put our loss behind us as we seek.
Guidance in the decisions ahead, feeling so weak.

Restore me again to feel God's presence within
Allowing myself to grieve the loss and let in
The peace that Jesus promised to all.
Who invite Him into our heart and accept His call?

RESTORATION

Restoration is a hard concept to grasp.
Done well, it will cause you to gasp.
Time and perseverance can get it right.
The results will offer a beautiful sight.

Restoration of a relationship is not an easy task.
Sometimes achieved, often we choose to don a mask.
Hiding our feelings, our attempts at repair to stop,
Lacking complete restoration, the relationship will drop.

Restoration of a feeling is hard to bring back.
Never fully realizing what we may lack.
We took a certain path that brought rewards.
A restoration of that path may be a way to move forwards.

A terrible storm may destroy our dwelling or house.
Seeking restoration from the storm may arouse.
Anxious moments from the storm's torments,
Seeking reasons for restorations' lack, we try another tack.

BOLDNESS

I have never considered myself bold.
I was often quiet and did what I was told.
I associated being bold with being brash.
Maybe even talking trash

I have a different view of boldness.
Speaking out with courage and bearing witness
What Jesus did while here on earth?
Knowing what He was to do, still going forth.

In many areas of the world, boldness is needed.
Doing work to combat oppression, the Word seeded.
In soil that was rocky and required care
Being a Christian, laying their life bare

Boldness in word and deed as a seed
If planted, it will not be overtaken by weeds.
Speaking out without fear
Because God is near

THE GROANING
OF THE EARTH

It is with trepidation that I hear a distant groaning.
I know it is my imagination that what I am hearing.
Although it is not happening, it catches my attention.
I find myself wondering why I feel such tension.

The groaning of the earth is in the change in temperature.
The fires and the droughts, the disregard for nature
We must pay attention, or we will lose the ability.
To make some changes to offer a new reality.

We cannot do it piecemeal or in small sections.
It has taken many years to get here with our actions.
Burying our heads in the sand, not wanting to acknowledge
Not heeding the warnings led by scientific knowledge.

The groaning of the earth will only get louder.
Until we can't ignore it, not feeling ourselves prouder.
In our accomplishments that at times hurt the earth
We must do better to show our actions have any worth

ANNIVERSARY OF
A TRAGEDY

Twenty-one years have passed since the tragedy in our history.
So much life was lost at a terrible cost; I find it a mystery.
How terrorists took that hate and attacked a nation
On many fronts, leaving a devastating situation.

There was a shocked nation that tried to understand.
The amount of destruction inflicted on our land.
A hand full of terrorists created so much damage.
Pitting one group of people against another

Lessons were learned and sadness remains years later.
Hate and bias may seem to win, but I won't be a hater!
At the very end, love will win as we pass from this life.
Into the life we are promised when we accept Jesus

Amid the tragedy, there were heroes.
Giving their life for another willingly
On this anniversary, I remember those heroes.
Concentrating on the unity throughout our nation

IN REMEMBRANCE

Throughout each year, days are celebrated in remembrance.
Yesterday, September Eleventh, was such a day, an instance.
Where one day changed a nation where hatred ruled
Brought on by the action of a few who were hatred fueled.

The minutes, hours, and days were spent trying to take in.
How those events could possibly happen.
Many lives were lost without any reason.
Except that a hatred brewed in this fall season

In our remembrance, we can move forward and change.
Letting go of all our anger, choosing to rearrange.
Our view towards others, innocent Muslims
Who were tainted by a few, calling themselves Muslims?

We can remember other times where hatred led.
Actions by a few to shed innocent blood fed.
By that hatred and lack of understanding
Knowing that at the end, love will be more commanding.

VISION OF TOMORROW

I hope my vision of tomorrow comes true.
A united America, celebrating the red, white, and blue.
A vision where unity amidst diversity shows through.
Where racism and bias, their presence withdrew

A vision of tomorrow where there is no oppression.
The understanding that true equality is a lesson.
We can learn and pay the concept our full attention.
We can listen closely, letting go of fear and apprehension.

A vision of tomorrow where hatred has lost its' grasp.
Violence is a thing of the past as we hold and clasp.
The belief that we can live together and experience peace.
Knowing that we will then have genuine release.

A vision of tomorrow where there is no division.
No need to hold the same beliefs or write a revision.
Of our prior history to sooth our guilt
Taking a new path to create a beautiful patchwork quilt.

GLIMPSES OF HEAVEN

Every so often, glimpses of heaven show up on Earth.
In the past two years, kindness to others has had a rebirth.
Paying it forward has become a common event.
Having an experience that seems to be heaven sent.

My own glimpses of heaven come in the wellness.
I feel as I live positively despite my mental illness.
I have felt peace and joy amidst stress and insecurity.
I live each day in the present, living in God's purity.

Glimpses of heaven in how others provide a hand up.
Reaching out to each other to offer a cup.
Of sustenance to lift the veil of selfishness
That divides us because of our willfulness.

Glimpses of heaven by ordinary people offering
Compassion and presence during a great suffering
Taking heroic measures to provide comfort and support.
Seeing the storms of life, no judging but providing a safe port

INJUSTICE

In the world, injustice finds a place.
It seems to be a problem within the human race.
Injustice comes in many forms.
At times, it appears injustice exists in all our norms.

How do we see injustice today?
Do we see it in the politics that come into play?
Is it present in what we say?
Can we find a new way?

Injustice will never disappear.
If we don't speak out without fear
Knowing we can act.
To no longer have injustice be a fact

Recognizing injustice is what I hope to do.
For I have a plan to show you
How we can make a difference
Not allowing injustice to have any endurance.

SILENCE

Silence is a two-edged sword.
If you agree, you don't say a word.
If you don't, you make a choice.
Not to courageously use your voice

Silence can set the tone.
Agreeing to something you don't condone.
You are going along with the crowd.
Because you fear to say how you feel out loud

Silence can allow you to listen and hear.
As you learn to listen not just with your ear
You can hear with your heart, tuning in
To the feelings underneath, above the din

Silence can speak volumes to show respect.
For a different point of view as you elect
To hear what is said and let another have a say.
Not to convince others to follow your way.

AN UNBENDING NATURE

If you have an unbending nature, you are unable to bend.
At times, many relationships can fail and end.
Broken fences which you are unable to mend.
Due to the way you see things and messages you send.

Trees that are unbending can't withstand the wind.
Unbending, they snap in half with no support to find.
If our views in life reflect our unbending nature,
We may experience an unpleasant future.

Only seeing issues as being black and white
Unable to bend and let in any brilliant light.
Shining into the recesses of our mind
Allowing sight of a different kind

An unbending nature can be reshaped to allow.
Change and provide a new path to follow.
Letting go of the past, unbending at last.
Seeing shades of grey with no more aspersions to cast

DECEPTION

I try very hard not to practice deception.
I recognize that I am no exception.
From this practice, especially on myself
I think it can be very easy to deceive yourself.

When I think I am well, both mentally and physically
I can deceive myself as I am unaware, totally.
Not seeing warning signs that indicate to me.
I am on a slippery slope and unable to see.

Deception can lead me down a path.
Either to mania or depression, leaving a swath.
Of brokenness that may fracture my health
Shaking my head in wonder at deceptions' stealth

It is only through an awareness of deception that I can.
Understand the power of deception, and maybe ban.
From my life, this practice of deception to take away.
The effect on me or have any kind of sway.

POWER

Power is not a bad thing, if used wisely
It is only when it is sought actively.
Over everything else, becoming most important.
This all-inclusive search is now your "soul" intent.

Power can be a potent desire.
Leading you astray with an all-encompassing fire
Never seeming to have enough power.
Igniting a fear causing many to cower

Power that recognizes the need for guidance
From above provides a better chance
To bring a balance so there is less corruption.
Choosing a more difficult path but showing gumption

God's power will always win.
We can fool ourselves by giving into sin.
Human power is not lasting.
God's power is everlasting.

ILLUSION

Having control of our life is often an illusion we have.
Thinking about comfort and monetary rewards can stave,
Off any feelings of not being worthy or enough
Giving up the illusion of control can be tough.

Many more illusions exist, like life being fair.
And those friends you have will show they care.
One major illusion is that, if you work hard.
To meet your goal, you can let down your guard.

There are many sayings to back up our illusion.
The early bird catches the worm is one version.
Chasing things like money and power can give.
The illusion that they are the reason to live.

Illusions exist in the world today concealing.
The truth and preventing the revealing.
That worldly rewards are fleeting.
Never preparing us for a heavenly greeting

A DECEPTIVE
APPEARANCE

I have often been told I appear outwardly calm.
In tough situations, that appearance may serve as a balm.
It is also a very deceptive appearance for I
Am anything but calm; my training is why.

A deceptive appearance can often play.
A pivotal role in what we do or say.
My training as a nurse has taught me.
To display a calmness for others to see

Emergencies cause my training to kick in.
Letting go of any nerves as I begin.
To do what I have been taught.
In circumstances that are danger fraught

A deceptive appearance can be good.
Judging wrongly, as I misunderstood
What a lesson God can give me
If it is just the outward appearance I see

IN TUNE

There are those who seem to march to a different beat.
They don't seek to blend in or stand out, giving a sweet
Melody that doesn't try to repeat in any way.
Out with the old, a new tune to play.

In tune with what is happening around
Listening closely to every sound
Hoping not to hear discord.
Which hate brings, love strikes a better chord.

In tune with others who support
Encouraging and providing a safe port
Singing in harmony, knowing a unity
Faith brings to give a community.

In tune with what God desires for us
Living with others with love as the focus
No longer blinded, loving the wrong things.
Seeing clearly the love that God brings

A CULTURE OF PRIVILEGE

What happens when a culture of privilege develops?
Seeing no need to strive, a sense of entitlement envelops.
Identifying wants as needs that are due.
Not because of anything you do

It is as if you belong to a class above all others.
Not being one who bothers
To work toward establishing a connection
Or doing anything with conviction

A culture of privilege seems to tear things apart.
Observing only differences, no unity to impart
No care or concern for another with division
Growing stronger, clouding a true vision

A culture of privilege goes directly against all.
That Jesus taught while here on earth, a pall.
Is cast upon those who embrace this culture.
To me they are no different than a vulture.

LEARNING

Romans 12:12 "Rejoice in hope; be patient in affliction; be persistent in prayer."

LESSONS LEARNED

When I think back over my life
I find the best lessons learned occur during strife.
My life may be proceeding on a positive note.
No trials, tribulations, or fiery dragons to smote.
It is only with some bumps in the road.
When I find myself under a heavy load
That those lessons learned in the past
May be dusted off and adapted to hold me fast.
Keeping me from being discouraged and giving in
Overcoming my situation, avoiding the din
Of all those voices erupting within
Trying to deter me from a possible win.
Letting those lessons learned save me again.

GRANDCHILDREN

A wonderful blessing is what grandchildren are.
They keep you young and energetic by far.
They broaden your views and provide cues.
On how to relate to the next generation
The future leaders of our nation
We can become unwilling to change.
It is important to make time to arrange.
Many dialogs that allow us to exchange
And maybe accept certain ideas that seem strange.
Foreign to our way of thinking
But providing a way of linking
Our generation to theirs
We might become joint heirs.
In undertaking projects to relieve the cares
Solving the problems made by man.
Helping the earth in every way we can

REPLENISH

We need to find a way to replenish our resources.
Needing to be aware of the results if no one forces
A rethinking of the way we use them without seeing.
What will happen, if we deplete all, to every human being?

We may fail to replenish our bodies with rest.
Resulting in exhaustion, sickness, and distress
We may fail to replenish water loss due to heat.
Finding ourselves dehydrated, feeling beat.

If the results of failing to replenish our bodies are so dire
Imagine what results to the Earth will be, a mire.
Of failing rivers unable to support life, becoming toxic.
Soil is no longer able to deliver edible food, which is also toxic.

A way to replenish our resources becomes more important.
Every day that passes without a doubt, revealing a portent
To show what will follow if we continue to delay.
We have to start in a serious way today.

FOLLOW THROUGH

Like a train crossing with lights and an arm
I have certain warning signals to disarm.
Keeping me safe from my mania if I display
Trouble with follow through, racing thoughts come into play.

I may start many projects at the same time.
If I have difficulty finishing them, it is a prime
Example of lack of follow through
A warning signal that mania is in full brew.

Follow through takes focus as well as drive.
When I cannot focus, I may still have to drive.
But driving is not enough to finish all my stuff.
Everything I am doing can disappear in a puff.

Follow through in actions and my thoughts.
Can serve to remind of coping aughts.
Not to get too committed in what I see and do.
If I can't follow through, it will not benefit you.

PRIORITIES

Priorities used to be difficult for me.
Trying to do and be a person everybody wanted me to be.
Realizing as I got older that lack of priorities hurt.
I became disillusioned, blaming myself for my failure to assert.

My bipolar journey has made me prioritize.
If I fail to do so, my mania will rise.
It is a spiral up if I don't realize.
All the commitments allow mania, my life to seize.

Priorities are easier if God is at my center.
I pray now before any commitments I enter.
This step makes my faith intentional.
My life now has much more potential.

No longer do I fear that mania will appear.
I am aware that the path I am on will tear.
Away my fears, giving me relief.
Further strengthening my belief

TOGETHER

There are many meanings for the word together.
It can be wholly integrated or, whether.
As a unified structure or balanced to accomplish
A task that could not be done alone, as in fulfilling a wish

The meaning that I feel is clear is to act jointly in a task.
It encompasses harmony, connection, relationship to bask.
In acceptance for who I am, not needing a mask.
Knowing that all I must do is reach out and ask.

Together, we can do so much more as the sum.
What we do with more than one offers a pleasant hum
Of cooperation in getting things done
Understanding that though we are many, we can act as one.

Together in action, we can change the world.
Christians in unity can make a better world.
We can take our differences and blend.
Providing an atmosphere for divisions to mend

THE CHALLENGE OF PERSEVERANCE

I know of no greater challenge than perseverance in life.
Continuing in difficult situations, riddled with strife.
Feeling a tension so thick you couldn't cut it with a knife.
Sorting through the obstacles that seem so rife.

Perseverance when the odds against success
Are greater than your ability to process.
All you would need to do is not make a mess.
But you continue as each failure you address.

Learning from each failure to never give up trying.
Every lesson you learn can help you in praying.
Open solutions so you eventually succeed.
Finding perseverance works to satisfy your need.

Perseverance builds up strength of character.
Proving to those who would choose to be a detractor.
What can be accomplished with perseverance?
Leaving absolutely nothing to chance

THERE IS HOPE

When there is trouble, I don't know what to do.
There is hope!
When I reach out to the One who provides a path to go
There is hope!

When I feel down, things look bleak.
There is hope!
When I fail to find what I seek
There is hope!

When I am faced with so much loss
There is hope!
When I can't sleep and continually toss
There is hope!

When I am traveling through a storm
There is hope!
When I think I'll never return to my norm
There is hope!

HEALTHY LIVING

Healthy living requires several steps to take.
The need for a new direction and decisions to make.
Allowing ourselves to believe that positive change.
Comes as we begin to examine what we need to rearrange.

What we eat, how we sleep, and amount of exercise
Make a huge difference on healthy living, I surmise.
Greater still is the effect of our outlook on life.
Do we bounce back from obstacles or give in to strife?

Do we listen to what our bodies say?
Are we determined to continue our way?
When our body says rest, do we continue without delay?
Taking a chance that we won't have a high price to pay.

Healthy living is a balanced life with equal amounts.
Of work and play as we realize everything we do counts
We can have peace, joy, and love within lifting us up.
Feeling that we have drunk from an overflowing cup.

GRACIOUS

Hoping to become a gracious person is a goal I have in mind.
I don't have to travel very far, for example, to find.
I have met quite a few people who seem to fit the bill.
In every way they show, it is a trait and a title they aptly fulfill.

In kindness, generosity, and tact, they are gracious to the core.
Making me desire to be a gracious person even more
Mercy and compassion also enter the mix.
I consider all I must do and any shortcomings I must fix.

Graciousness is a very acceptable Christian trait.
I hope that I have the patience and ability to wait.
Knowing I have more to do to accomplish this goal.
Before my body gives out and I hear the death knoll

Being gracious can be an enormous task.
Taking the time to listen to what others may ask.
Lending a hand to friends and strangers alike
Never passing judgement or telling them to take a hike.

A HEART FILLED
WITH GRATITUDE

It is the designated day to have a heart full of gratitude.
I think it would be wonderful if we had this attitude.
Every day of the year, never failing to see what we have.
Recognizing those before us and what they gave

A heart filled with gratitude will start each day.
In a positive manner so there is no way
For my day to start with a feeling of sorrow
Fretting about what may happen tomorrow.

A heart filled with gratitude will prepare.
Me so that everything I have I will share.
I know this to be the Christian way.
Able to intentionally think about what I say.

With gratitude in my heart, I also experience joy.
Akin to a child's reaction to a new toy
My steps reflect the joy in my heart as they buoy.
My body up for the activities of the day with joy

A NEED FOR CONNECTION

The pandemic has brought attention to the need for connection.
Technology has helped, but it's not the same as interaction.
Personal touch and face to face is so different to me.
There is a better ability to reach out and to see.

A need for connection can start a conversation.
A way to build a bridge and offer persuasion.
We can speak to each other without fear.
Creating a dialog to understand and bring us near

A need for connection is part of our humanity.
It offers a way to protect our sanity.
No longer locked into ourselves so much
That we act on our own and lose touch

A need for connection is evident as we fellowship together.
Bringing out the best of us as we work as one whether.
We totally agree, but we see the worth of each person.
Sharing our talents, making this time in life our best season

A LASTING LOVE

A marriage with a lasting love is beyond measure.
I view it as a wonderful gift I will always treasure.
Not easy to sustain and maintain a balance.
It may appear to be effortless at first glance.

Lasting love requires constant care.
Taking love for granted is not an action you dare.
To make, as life brings challenges to that love.
It takes words and actions that love to prove.

Lasting love with give and take to see.
The need of each to blend and be.
In harmony to build a life together
Helping all difficulties to weather

Lasting love is never demanded or takes for granted.
Work done by each one to provide what's wanted.
Putting the needs of the other and fulfilling their role.
Uplifting to prevent obstacles from taking a toll.

DREAMS FULFILLED

Some dreams change, some are fulfilled.
Changed dreams are not God willed.
My dream of becoming a nurse came true.
Years later, it's as if the time flew.

Years of education and practice passed by
New areas of nursing to notice and try.
Goals at the beginning are not always kept.
Seeing new opportunities to which I leapt

Dreams fulfilled leave no regrets.
Life has been as good as it gets.
Opportunities came to me.
At the right time for me to see

Dreams fulfilled are good memories.
Wishing at times that I could freeze.
That moment in time to relive.
Those times I felt most alive.

WHAT IS INTEGRITY?

Many attributes are present in personal integrity.
It encompasses honor and commitment to the nitty gritty.
The ability to see a complete picture, not just a part.
Doing all that needs to be done with your whole heart.

Integrity means not making promises you can't keep.
Understanding that your word can offer a deep
Connection to help others realize they are not alone.
Helping to handle difficulties to which they are prone.

Integrity is seen when words and actions match.
No hidden meanings or agendas to catch.
A helping hand when obstacles are met.
Knowing what you see is what you get.

Integrity reveals a life lived with respect.
For what is right and good and to reject,
A selfish life filled with neglect.
On a path that leads to hurt and regret

POSSIBILITIES

When I allow negative thoughts in
I turn them around.
To look at possibilities within
I can rebound.

Possibilities abound.
Too many I have found.
I must pick and choose.
Hoping no opportunity to lose

Letting myself think outside the box.
To see what it unlocks
Realizing that possibilities are limitless.
To not do anything would be pointless.

Possibilities give life meaning.
Making strides I can't believe.
No longer am I backward leaning.
Seeing possibilities, all anxiety I do relieve.

FINDING CALM AMIDST THE STORM

There are moments where I feel buffeted by storms.
It is in those moments that a solution forms.
Remembering the calm that my faith provides
Brings me to the peace that only in God resides.

Finding calm amidst the storm, I depend
On the Son, Jesus, that God did send.
Spending time in devotion and prayer
Provides me with a protective layer.

Finding hope within the storm only comes
When I turn all over to Him who welcomes
Me as a child and sends me strength to survive.
All the hardships in the storm, I can revive.

Finding calm amidst the storm gives me courage.
To carry on while around me the storm may rage.
It is in the storms that my faith does grow.
As the blessings God gives, I come to know.

*PERSISTENCE

Persistence and stubbornness are related.
One has a negative connotation when stated.
Being stubborn can be looked at and judged.
To be a character flaw, never to be budged

Persistence is seen more positively.
As hanging in and pursuing actively
Getting what you want, not giving up.
As you proceed to give yourself a full cup.

Sometimes being an optimist goes along.
With persistence as you believe you can bring
About what you are trying to achieve
Not willing to accept failure and leave.

Persistence implies a willingness to
Continue trying but able to know.
When it is not possible to do
Move on, recognizing when to go.

STRESS

Stress never has a good effect.
Often leading me to suspect
If I found a better way
To handle it, good health would stay.

When I give in to stress
I really must confess.
Life can become a mess.
Leaving me with much less

Stress leaves me unable to
Handle all the things I need to do.
Overwhelmed by what I am feeling.
Finding myself appealing

Seeking ways to cope
Trying to find hope.
Keeping stress at bay
Putting good methods into play

BUILDING BLOCKS

All those experiences in life
Are building blocks, learning how to handle strife.
Some learning is hard.
Leaving pieces of life, like broken glass in a shard

Infancy, where all your needs are met.
Childhood, where dependence we forget.
Adulthood, where we may feel regret.
Old age, knowing what we begat.

Building blocks all along
Getting us to where we belong
Often wishing we didn't get it wrong.
Sometimes, we traveled with the throng.

MOMENTUM

Life may take on a momentum beyond what we conceive.
Lifting us up so many milestones we achieve
Plans change with life turning out differently, I believe.
Letting go of past dreams; regrets I can relieve.

Momentum increases my pace.
Running as if in a race
I must not let it get out of hand.
Or else I will have little energy to stand.

It is in balance I must live.
Knowing that mania will give.
No opportunity to gradually slow down
I will instead crash, feeling about to drown.

Momentum with balance is what I strive for
It is an important concept at the core.
Of how I live my life today
Recognizing it is the best way.

INTERDEPENDENT

We choose to look at dependent and independent.
Rarely, looking at the term interdependent
There are times in life where we are dependent.
Toddlers, as they grow, become more independent.

As we grow older, we find ourselves more dependent.
Do we consciously choose to be interdependent?
God gives us special gifts and talents.
We use interdependently as a balance.

Our culture may stress independence.
Our faith stresses interdependence
Though there are many of us, we can act as one.
Knowing Jesus, we have won.

A life with peace and harmony
Fostering unity in our diversity
Letting interdependence be the rule
So, pride in self can no longer fool.

LACKING CONFIDENCE

It is hard to see when I am lacking confidence.
I may overachieve to provide a sense.
Of confidence that I do not feel
Pretending I am confident for real.

Lacking confidence can reflect.
Past experiences and detect.
A harsh criticism given in the past
With continuing effects that last

Lacking confidence can cast doubt.
That I can do something about
The situation I find myself in
Causing me to feel I cannot win.

Lacking confidence can be turned around.
If I turn to God, I have found.
He gives me confidence to do a job.
Feeling an accomplishment that the Devil can't rob.

MOTIVATION

John 11:25 Jesus said to her, "I am the resurrection and the life. The one who believes in me, even if he dies, will live."

HIDDEN TALENTS

Some of us let fear derail us.
Hidden talents remain hidden thus.
Never exploring deeper to see what lays.
Below the surface so hidden it stays

Playing it safe, no challenge to seek
Doing what is expected and unwilling to peek.
As time goes on and hidden talents stay
Buried, failing to come into play.

Hidden talents, when they surface.
Can be developed to serve God's purpose.
Making a difference in the world to uncover
A better tomorrow as they help us recover.

Hidden talents can be the answer to move.
Mountains that seem impossible, but with love
Applied to each situation, those hidden talents.
Can indeed provide a God infused balance.

SEEKING TO OVERCOME

In our history, seeking to overcome is an anthem.
A journey traveled by those oppressed by "them."
Every immigrant who comes to find a better life.
Escaping from countries at war, bringing great strife

It is a present for those brought here, not on their own.
Laborers, some with skills to hone
Indentured servants or slaves to serve a master.
Some can escape their circumstances faster.

Always seeking to overcome
The label was put on them by some.
Seeking to overcome loss of self-esteem.
Finding it so difficult, wanting to scream

Seeking to overcome lack of understanding.
Or escape the labels which were branding.
Seen as unequal or having less standing.
No respect by others, commanding

TAKING ORDINARY INTO EXTRA-ORDINARY

Staying ordinary is what we ask.
Unable or unwilling to do the task.
God asks of us.
Wanting to avoid the fuss.

Taking the ordinary into extra-ordinary needs trust
Accomplishing that which God says we must.
Letting go of the reasons we can't.
Instead going ahead, good things to plant

Taking the ordinary into the extra-ordinary honors
A God who enables us to do, not be one who ponders.
Not being one who is self-willed.
Acting as a person who is God willed.

Taking the ordinary into the extra-ordinary gives
Hope to others who see a Christian who dives.
Into action led by God to do something beyond
What can be done alone, but to God we respond.

EMBRACING THE UNKNOWN

Embracing the unknown is not an easy feat.
We seek to know what is ahead and walk to a familiar beat.
Stepping out into the unknown makes a heart race.
Not anything we want to embrace.

Embracing the unknown can be the start.
Of a lifelong adventure we follow with all our heart
Letting go of fear to trust God's guidance.
As we take steps in a new life dance

Embracing the unknown can be a chance.
To choose ways that may enhance.
Our life as new experiences we seek.
No longer feeling fearful and weak.

Embracing the unknown lets us.
Leave behind the anxiety and fuss.
Because we lack trust to step out
Of the shadow of fear and in victory, shout

CHARACTER BUILDING

There are some things I do that are ways.
To build character so that in future days
I can look back to see how far I have come.
A better-balanced person I have become.

Character building never stops.
It may lay dormant until it grows.
Up in a situation that requires.
A change that allows you to uncross wires.

Character building may occur at any time.
In life, not just while you are in your prime
Early days, before school, parents may
Stress certain attributes by what they say.

Later, it may be a job that will.
Build character and fulfill.
My purpose found in life to lead.
As I am offered many ways to succeed

TIME

I find time confusing, either passing quickly or dragging on
As I grow older, it seems that time is a blur and gone.
The good times I want to hold for longer than I can.
Even those bad times in the past that I thought I outran.

Time is not something that is easily managed.
It gets away from me, leaving me damaged.
Because I don't get to redo what is past
Wishing to have done one thing that will last.

Time that is wasted in frivolous activities again.
Doing many things without any gain
Learning that time is more valuable as I grow older.
Wanting to do more and in my actions, be bolder.

When I was young, I didn't think about time.
Doing nothing with my time now seems like a crime.
Wishing I knew then what I know now leaves a regret.
I can't change so I will choose to accept and forget.

WORDS THAT UPLIFT

I am trying very hard to use words that uplift.
Words said in anger, causing pain and a rift.
Words not thought out, unable to call back.
Words that move others away and me off track

Words can uplift or not in the way you speak.
A note of judgement can sometimes sneak.
Into words that you say to do the opposite
As these words are not what you wish to posit

I wonder, if I stop to pray, before I speak aloud
Finding words that honor God and not the crowd.
How I would feel, would I feel proud?
I hope I will not, but simply no longer cowed.

Thinking before I talk as I choose my words.
I can uplift and move forwards.
In my walk and continue to grow more mature
In my faith, taking on a more Christian nature.

REJUVENATE

Our culture emphasizes "staying young."
As if growing old, leaves us feeling less strong.
There is a slew of products to rejuvenate.
Trying to avoid the signs age may generate.

Magic elixirs, face lifts, are used to stay young.
We seem to be stressing age with youth among
The most desirable attributes while trying hard.
Denying any good when we play the aging card.

Rejuvenate means to make young again or restore.
Accepting that meaning, not looking for more
Limits our thinking and fails to look deep.
Not able to see what beauty and wisdom we keep.

Rejuvenate is having a certain vigor.
Preventing me from standing still in rigor
Fighting age is a no-win situation.
Leading to a great deal of frustration

CHERISH

Knowing God's love is something I cherish.
He keeps me on the right road, so I don't perish.
So many temptations in the world today
I can resist all with God as I pray.

Knowing the one I cherish also cherishes me.
Allowing me to see the kind of person I can be.
He gives me freedom to choose a better way.
Resting in His arms today and every day

I cherish the man I married, feeling I have won.
The best prize of all, God gave me.
A wonderful life, so many memories to see.
We will soon celebrate forty-eight years as one.

The song "Cherish" is our song.
Popular when we were young.
I took the path God put me upon
Seeing us through the hard times until done

RIGHT TIME AND PLACE

There are moments when I look back.
I see a definite pattern and track.
Unaware, at the time, why God put me there.
Discovering later, it was to show God's care.

Those times occur when I give control away.
To God who leads me as I obey
He takes me to a time and place.
Allowing me to show His grace.

Many wonderful things come about.
And make me want to shout.
God leads me to the right time and place.
To do His will; my will gone without a trace

Starting the day with God and prayer
Adds a much deeper layer.
My plan for the day He may replace.
Using me at the right time in the right place

ACCEPTANCE

There is so much meaning in this one word.
Acceptance holds a valued place to move toward
We want to feel acceptance for who we are.
Wanting others to see what we have done so far.

Acceptance may be for a stance we hold.
Taking a chance to step out and be bold.
An occurrence we don't want to face.
Hoping it will disappear without a trace.

Acceptance is not easy to address.
It can cause us to feel stress.
Feeling God's love can change me.
Not desiring acceptance to see

God's love allows me to accept myself.
Putting the need for acceptance on a shelf
Going forward and feeling free
To let myself just be

THE HEALING POWER
OF HUMOR

In the healing process, humor helps to bounce back.
Helping take the edge off the situation and attack.
Stress and to provide a way to diffuse.
Any anger at the situation, putting it to good use.

Humor can help us to relax so we can hear.
Clearly what is said without the interference of fear.
Humor leads to a positive outlook that can aid.
In enabling us to allow all negativity to fade

The healing power of humor has become an interest.
As medical science shows with articles, needing study to test.
The ability of humor to change the outcome.
Finding methods of using humor in treatments to come

In my own life, I know humor has been important.
Overcoming mental illness to a great extent
I can see the humor in situations that in the past
Have bothered me, but they no longer hold fast.

WITHOUT YOU IN MY LIFE

Without you in my life, I would be lacking.
So many good things no longer tracking.
My feelings may have developed over time.
But over the years, they continued to climb.

Without you in my life, I would be missing.
The wonderful way I feel when we are kissing.
The love I feel has only increased.
Knowing it has never ceased.

Without you in my life, I would feel half of a whole.
Feeling incomplete would take its' toll.
Talking things out has helped me to see.
A different side of things, becoming a better me.

Without you in my life, there would be a hole.
In my heart, and many an incomplete goal
The things I have achieved.
Have been because, in me, you believed.

WHAT TRUE FRIENDSHIP
LOOKS LIKE

If you have been lucky enough to have a true friend
You know that there isn't anything to make it end.
That friend is honest with you, it is you they will protect,
If any difficulty or danger, they detect.

True friendship requires sacrifice of self.
Putting all that may interfere on a shelf.
It requires shared confidences that stay.
Between friends, never to betray.

True friendship is one where you can depend.
When times are rough, it will not bend.
Or break, but it will strengthen.
The ties that hold it together will lengthen.

True friendship can last a lifetime.
You must be open to it as it would be a crime.
To live a lifetime without a true friend
Who can often help our ways to mend?

A LIFE OF SERVICE

I hope that the life I lead is a life of service.
One where I address need and serve a purpose.
A life of service to demonstrate love and care.
God gave to me so that love I could share.

I witnessed firsthand that kind of life displayed.
By my mother and mother-in-law, who played.
A role of Christian mentorship for me to see.
What a life of service could truly be

Giving with no expectation of return
Being open to others and to learn
How best to serve them, treating all
As equals when answering God's call.

A life of service, shown by Jesus, is my desire.
Deepening my walk with God, taking me higher
Lighting in me a burning fire, so I can serve.
Fully with no doubt, not willing to swerve.

WHOSE AUTHORITY

On whose authority do I reflect?
Is it my way to deflect?
Choosing the way of the world so I neglect
The true authority which I should respect.

Authority of the world will not hold.
A new authority will always arise.
Who will be new and bold?
Hoping to walk away with the prize.

Whose authority will hold true to the end?
It will never, ever break or bend.
God has authority that is true.
He turned us into a being that is new.

Trusting in His authority gives us purpose.
While here on Earth, we are in His service.
Even if we don't accept without question,
He still lifts us up in each life's section.

FIRST STEPS

Our first steps are taken with hesitance.
Often with an unsure stance
Practice gives us a better chance.
Of becoming sure footed so we can prance

Faith steps may follow the same path.
Initially we may focus on God's wrath.
As we read and learn, we come to see His love.
The stories in the Bible become a treasure trove.

As we grow, those first steps lead.
And give us the encouragement we need.
Our understanding expands.
God holds us in His hands.

The first steps are important at the start.
Of a lifelong journey where we will be a part
Being a Christian and showing in our heart
Nothing in this world can split us apart.

LIFE'S INTERRUPTIONS

Sometimes it is in those moments, the places where,
Life's interruptions may take you over there.
Not where you intended to be but to a place.
So different, offering you growth in a new space.

Life's interruptions, when allowed to play out.
May give you reasons, in joy, to shout.
Finding, in life, a new purpose
Enabling new talents to surface

Life's interruptions offer more than we can see.
It can be the way God leads us so that we
Follow the path He has planned for us.
We can choose to follow or to fuss.

In those interruptions, we can envision.
An entirely new and fulfilling mission.
To take us to places we have never been.
Witnessing things, we would never have seen.

OUT OF FOCUS

At times, my life goes out of focus.
Unable to determine my true locus.
A plan that fails to work to move.
In a way where I can find my groove

Out of focus because of distraction
Or pursuing a wrong action
A way to refocus is to step back.
Look at where I am and what I lack.

Out of focus can cause a crack.
In my protective armor, unable to track.
Where things went wrong
Feeling very weak, not strong

Out of focus may let my bipolar take over.
Finding I must take cover.
Or else I may find a life that is upside down.
Leaving me wearing a frown

ONE ON ONE WITH
THE ONE

I find there are times when I fail to start my day.
Not one on one with the one who leads the way.
Those days do not go well, walking blind.
Without the sight brought by God to my mind

I feel disjointed and unsure of what I am to do.
Because I do not have God's plan so
I wander aimlessly without focus, not knowing.
Whether this day will be faith growing

When I am one on one with the one
Who brought me into being, gone.
Is the lack of connection that keeps,
Me from feeling down as my strength seeps.

I do not want to lose that one on one.
With the One who chooses me and won
My redemption at the cross
So, my life is not a loss.

*RESURRECTION #2

As Easter approaches, many thoughts turn to resurrection.
We see the light that replaces the darkness of the crucifixion.
It is the resurrection of the church at the forefront.
Of our thoughts, facing a situation that seems to daunt.

We find ourselves dwindling in number every year.
Hoping to turn around the situation amidst fear.
As we see churches failing in their mission to bring
People coming to know Jesus, his praises to sing.

Resurrection means rising to life from death.
Churches appear to be going from life to death.
How can resurrection occur if we depend on man?
Only God can resurrect, no one person can.

As churches divide, taking too much of the world.
In so our faith loses its' flavor and hurled
About with the politics of man, so polarized
Resurrection by God must be prioritized.

THEME

Isaiah 40:30-31 "Youths may become faint and weary, and young men may stumble and fall, but those who trust in the Lord will renew their strength; they will soar on wings like eagles; they will run and not grow weary; they will walk and not grow faint."

EXALTED

Very rarely do we see the word exalted used.
In normal conversation as we are confused
About its' meaning, although it is used frequently.
In the Bible as it is applied to God specifically

The Bible uses glorify interchangeably with exalt.
If I wish to exalt another human, I will halt.
Because I would make an idol in this way
That is not something I would do or say.

I think of exalted as being highly praised
Above everyone, elevated and raised.
I know of no human I would exalt today.
I can think of two who have passed away.

Billy Graham and Queen Elizabeth were those two.
They sought to exalt the Lord, not to be who.
Chose to be exalted in any way, seeking to
Lead others to witness a loving God to get to know.

HOME IS NOT A PLACE

I have discovered home is not a place.
It is not a defined space.
It can change or stay the same.
It may be called by a certain name.

To me, home is where my heart is.
It is the loved ones present and those I miss.
I have lived in many houses over the years.
Some became home as I left with many tears.

Someday in the future, I will have a forever home.
Spending an eternity under a heavenly dome
What will tomorrow bring or who will come?
I just know while here, I must say welcome.

ADVENT: A HOPE RENEWED

Being busy is part of the season of Advent.
It can take away the meaning of this blessed event.
Stopping to reflect on this season of hope.
Gives us an ability to prioritize and cope.

This time of the year brings hope renewed.
Seeing the birth of Christ that was viewed.
By shepherds and the animals in the manger
An environment that sometimes seems stranger

It takes time to discover the meaning.
Of the humble beginning of Jesus birth
Each time, reading the Gospel, we get a gleaning.
Families brought together to celebrate with mirth.

A humble beginning with lowly shepherds
Allows us to see how much God loves us.
In His actions, not just His words
The birth of Jesus without a great deal of fuss

GREETING THE SEASON WITH JOY AND PEACE

I am greeting the season with joy and peace.
Taking time to reflect and for activities to cease.
Avoiding the tension which busyness brings
Resting in His love, my heart sings

Remembering Jesus is the reason for the season.
Letting all the worldly activities breeze on
Without my presence as I choose to lose myself
Placing all other considerations on the shelf

Greeting the season with joy and peace brings release.
No rushing here and there, I experience His peace.
The joy of the season is not overshadowed.
By dwelling on receiving, giving generously is allowed.

The joy and peace of Christmas can stay through the year.
If I truly celebrate, His presence takes away all fear.
I know the special meaning of being His child.
Seeking to live life humbly, to be meek and mild.

THE GREATEST GIFT

There are many good gifts received in this season.
The greatest gift is Jesus, the reason for the season.
Gifts break or go out of style, no longer used or useful.
The greatest gift lasts forever for which I am grateful.

Jesus is the gift of hope, love, joy, and peace.
Overwhelming gratitude without cease
The trappings of Christmas will never last
Only Jesus offers us forever, if we hold fast.

The greatest gift is offered freely.
Without any strings, but fully
Paid for with God's love.
Flowing down from Heaven above

Holding fast to the true meaning
Christmas offers, so I find myself forward leaning.
As I listen to the words of hymns
Written to provide hope to one who sins.

WRAPPED IN HIS PRESENCE

Christmas can be so busy, the distractions so great.
Shopping, decorating, and trying to create.
That special feeling as we celebrate the season.
Doing unnecessary activities as we forget the reason.

Instead of wrapping presents this year.
I am wrapped in His presence and held near
Feeling so deeply the reason for the season
Allowing all the busyness to pass on.

Wrapped in His presence gives me relief.
No longer pursuing things that give me grief.
The hustle and bustle which can take away.
Joy of the season as my temper may fray.

Wrapped in His presence allows me to see.
The true meaning of Christmas and be.
Present in His presence every day
Grounded in His word as I pray.

A NEW YEAR ARRIVES

Each new year begins with anticipation and a plan.
Turning over a new leaf or meeting a goal, if you can
Putting so much pressure on yourself can take away.
The joy of starting off with a clean slate on the first day

A new year arrives with resolutions made.
All the preparations for a good year have been laid.
Excitement and expectations of what lies ahead.
Serve to keep negative thoughts away instead.

As the new year arrives, we turn away from the past
Hoping that the plans we make now will last.
Often forgetting to pace ourselves as we race.
Trying to leave last year behind without a trace.

MATURING IN FAITH

Nourishment enables growth in body and soul.
This year, to mature in my faith, is my goal.
Each day will be time spent in thy word.
Having joy in this new chapter, as I move forward.

Maturing in faith requires commitment to see.
Where time spent with God will take me
Answering the call, as I am led by Him.
Seeing the difference between it and a whim

Maturing in faith opens eyes and heart.
To see opportunities to do His will for a start.
Placing a priority on His will, not mine
Will allow my life to work out fine.

WELCOMING A NEW LIFE

A baby is born, and a new life begins.
A family grows into being with signs.
That a new generation is forming
As the world continues transforming

A new life brings new sensations.
With so many presentations
Gifts given for a new arrival.
As parents are so tired, they need revival.

The scramble to get ready takes a toll.
Each day will bring a need to set a goal.
To set the right path to travel on
Before that course is forever gone

A new life with an ability to shape and take.
New steps to provide a good foundation and make.
A future generation, better equipped to handle.
Praying to seek God's light as we light candle.

*TRUST IS MY WORD TO LIVE BY

I picked a word to live by for the year.
I chose trust and plan to put it into gear.
Stepping out in faith and letting go of control.
Allowing God to determine where I troll.

Trust in myself as I learn to discern.
I intentionally seek His Will and turn.
Away from all those unnecessary tasks
No longer hiding and wearing masks.

Trust in the path I take to travel on
Wishing that all doubts would be gone.
Praying with each step I take
A difference in this world I will make.

Trust that all will work as God plans.
It will be His plans and not mans.
Knowing that worry equals lack of trust.
Giving up worry is a must.

LED

Over the years, I have been led.
By His words, I have been fed.
Beautiful things I have heard.
Listening to hymns based on His words.

Led by the Holy Spirit
To stand and commit
To do His will
His work to fulfil.

Led by voices from my past.
A powerful witness they cast.
Seeing how their faith did last.
Enabled me to hold mine fast.

Led by His force.
That set my course.
To follow His way
I plan to continue every day.

SPIRIT LED

I have witnessed a few people who are spirit led.
Nourished by the Holy Bible; they are well fed.
Prayer for them is as important as breathing.
Each day they pray without ceasing.

They seem to see God's presence everywhere.
Offering kind words, in everything they share
Seeing others as God sees them, not judging.
Acting in such a manner, you see God's nudging.

Spirit led in every way, disciples on display.
I pray that as I mature, I will slay.
All the self-centered, selfish ways at play
And let the spirit hold sway.

Following wherever the spirit leads
Not giving into those bad seeds
Of doubt and mistrust that lead me astray
A true Christian, not just one I portray.

IN THE WORLD, NOT
OF THE WORLD

Striving to understand and discern the Word.
I wonder at my inability to see, but it occurred.
That God's timing had a part to play.
Maybe there was a reason for the delay.

In the world, not of the world is on my mind.
God put the thought there so I could find.
Understanding the world can cause pain.
Not looking to myself to overcome is a gain.

I am not alone in the world, you see.
Jesus overcame it for you and me.
I am not the center of my world.
The messages of the Bible have unfurled.

Having God at the center of all I do
It is His Word that I can sow.
As I live in this world, but view.
A greater one I will eventually go to

STANDING UP FOR FAITH

Faith needs action to demonstrate its' power.
The person who stands up for faith is a tower.
Displaying what God can do through our faith.
We need His strength to withstand man's wraith.

Standing up for faith means speaking out.
As an injustice occurs, using our voices to shout.
Knowing that only when we take a stand.
Can we change what is happening in our land?

Standing up for faith requires courage.
There may be stiff opposition with rage.
Poured out against, but God's presence.
Will give us a peace that we sense.

Standing up for faith is a way to grow.
In being a disciple, God's love to show
Knowing there is nothing we can do on our own.
But faith in action shows we have grown.

CHOOSING WISE WORDS

Speaking without thinking is never wise.
There are words to be used in a concise
Manner, intending to edify and uplift.
Not to put down or give a negative drift.

Choosing wise words is a talent, I hope.
To develop, learning to be quiet and cope
By not putting my foot in my mouth
Saying the wrong words, being uncouth

Trying to be quick to listen, slow to speak.
It may be misinterpreted as being weak.
But what you speak you can't take back
Those words may show the wisdom you lack.

Choosing wise words can shut off anger.
Throwing words back cause anger to linger
Knowing when to speak those wise words.
Is something I heartily move towards.

KNOWING JESUS

Learning about Jesus is not the same as knowing.
No real relationship developing or growing.
Do we think he is a character in the Bible?
Admittedly, there is no other character to rival.

Knowing Jesus is the Son of God is the start.
Of the building a relationship, but only part
We must choose to lose our life by putting.
Him first, all desires not Christlike cutting

Knowing Jesus and His love changes me.
All the selfishness will flee.
Because Jesus lives inside for all to see
Leading by His example, a disciple to be

Knowing Jesus leads me to share.
His love and good news to bear.
As I follow Him, I gain a new vision.
Of unity, no longer seeing division.

TIME SET ASIDE

Life gets too busy for me.
Cluttered with so much to do.
Not setting aside time for God so
I need to slow down, His wonders to see.

Time set aside to abide.
With each other, turning the tide.
Moving forward humbly, without pride
I can witness life's softer side.

Time set aside to find rest.
Striving to do my best.
Letting go and choosing zest.
Of life, no longer keeping abreast.

Time set aside to achieve a balance.
Between work and play, seeing a chance.
To reduce all anxiety and stress
Aware of all God does to bless.

A SABBATH FRAME
OF MIND

I consider Sabbath a day of rest.
Where I give God my very best
A Sabbath frame of mind
As I cease my daily grind

A Sabbath frame of mind takes.
A conscious effort and makes.
A difference in my life as I know.
Trusting God to provide is the way to go.

A Sabbath frame of mind can happen every day.
If I stop and choose to go His way
I will find peace of mind to say.
I am having a wonderful today.

A Sabbath frame of mind honors the One.
Who created me, as well as the Son.
It is not just a day I forget work.
A time with God where no distractions lurk.

QUALITIES

Acts 2:17 "And it will be in the last days, says God, that I will pour out my Spirit on all people; then your sons and your daughters will prophesy, your young men will see visions, and your old men will dream dreams."

ALONE

Alone is not where I want to be.
Alone is not what is best for me.
Alone is a place I go.
Alone is not a place to grow.
Alone is a feeling of emptiness and despair.
Alone allows me to feel there is no one to care.
Alone can lead me to depression.
Alone does not let my fears lessen.
Alone is a way to isolate.
Alone refuses to help me relate.
Alone can color my view.
Alone keeps me from seeing things anew.
But wait, I am not alone.
I can use my phone.
DBSA is there!
And they do care!

WHOLE

There are times in my life.
When I have felt strife
Often, I feel that I have missing parts.
I have many false starts.
As I try to again feel whole
It is like I am at the base of a knoll.
Fighting my way up, not looking down
Trying to find a smile and not frown.
Refusing to allow sadness to win.
Putting on a new skin
As I am once again whole

CHOICE

There are so many things in which we have a choice.
We can remain silent or use our voice.
We can choose to follow the crowd.
Or we can take a different stance and be proud.
What we do and how we do it can frame
The life we live and the beliefs we claim.
Decide carefully in the choices you make.
Those choices will impact the path you take.
They may define you as a follower or leader.
Viewed as being strong or weaker.

LONGEVITY

I come from a long line of long-lived women.
Strong women of faith with one thing in common
A spirit of giving, an independence balanced by
Their dependence on God; willing to try.
To follow where God led
Many times, allowing that spirit to be fed.
By a community of others sharing
The presence of God, not caring
What trials were faced in their life?
If God was present amidst the strife.

RECOGNITION

A pat on the back or simple thank you.
May address any lack by providing a few.
Acknowledgements of a job well done
To show that I have gone above and beyond.
What was expected of me, and I respond
Allowing the recognition to wash over me.
Knowing that others can see.
The time and the effort put forth by me.
But I hope the recognition I seek is not at all.
The reason for what I do or else I will fall.
Into a trap of self-serving, thereby swerving.
From the person I hope to be
A quiet person whose actions no-one will see.
God gets the recognition and not me.

AWAKENING

The sun rises brilliantly in my awakening.
Colors seem much brighter in my reckoning.
I am learning to be more aware.
Seeking ways in which to share
I take more time for myself to absorb.
All the many changes present in this orb
The earth is not stagnant, nor is it just a fragment.
It is a major part of my life as I enjoy creation.
All the many wonders in this current station
Awakening to all that I have been missing.
By not spending time and listening
To all the sounds of nature I strain to hear
Seeing all the beauty my eyes can bear.
I find myself in a season of awakening.

*VISION

I sit and contemplate the many meanings of the word vision.
To focus my mind as I make a decision.
About the best way to mold them into a fusion
As I lessen their number to eliminate confusion.
Vison is not just seeing.
Nor is it just the dream of being.
There are so many facets of the word.
It is very hard to find an accord.
In how we define the meaning
Without somehow leaning
Toward a narrowing understanding of vision
Therefore, I am making it my mission.
To examine vison boards, statements, and second sight
Shining a spiritual light, finding an answer to this plight
Vision is being allowed to see and be the best me.

BALANCE

Each year in my Bipolar journey
Balance becomes more important.
Enabling me to see the way.
Balance is a concept that is not distant.
To my recovery of who I used to be
A me not quite the same, I see.
But one who is stronger than before.
Recognizing who I am at the core.
There will never be a perfect balance.
Although I know I have a better chance
Of a more contented life for me
Seeking a balance to which I can agree.

LISTENING CLOSELY

Hearing such music takes me back.
To a time when I could enjoy, not lack.
The ability to see and hear music.
That brought back precious memories.

Listening closely, I can find.
A peace that comes to me, a kind
Of gentle touch comes to my memory
As I feel a temporary pleasure

Listening closely, I close my eyes.
I feel the gentle roll of the sea.
I can remember the wonderful lights in the skies.
The music takes me to a different place to see.

Listening closely, I am lost.
No longer dwelling on the cost.
The many moments that have passed
Spending time in busy work, failing to enjoy the sounds of the past

STRIVING

There are many things for which I am striving.
In certain moments, I realize I am not thriving.
I continue in my journey, unable to stop.
Until I reach the point where my focus will drop

I am striving on my own too often.
Unwilling to really see how to soften.
My continual striving for the wrong things
Leads me to a place where my soul fails to sing.

I am slowly learning that God must lead my striving.
If He is in charge, the force that is driving.
My striving will lead to the right thing.
Making my heart, mind, and soul sing

Now when I am striving with God in charge.
I know that He will lead me well and recharge.
My strength and energy so I can realize.
What I am striving for is the ultimate prize.

ABIDING

I choose a few words to use, even though I fail to grasp their meaning.
One of these words has been in my vocabulary a long time, abiding.
Abiding has quite a few definitions, but one seems a better fit for me.
To abide is to remain stable or fixed in a state, the way I long to be.

Abiding also means to endure or withstand.
With a diagnosis of Bipolar, I do understand.
There are times in my journey that I did endure.
Making the trek with steps that were often unsure.

The other definitions also apply to my situation.
To wait for or to accept without objection.
It has been a long process as I travel the road.
To a recovery from symptoms that add a great load

I can choose to be abiding in faith that I can be stable.
Rising well above any difficulty ahead or the label
Of mental illness, not allowing the stigma to hold me back.
Or choosing to believe that there is anything I lack.

STUCK

In life, there are times when I feel stuck.
Unable to move forward, trying to duck.
From the effects of experiences in the past
Seeing the dark shadows, they cast

Stuck in a previous time with an inability to move.
With a feeling of dejection that I will fail to prove
I can overcome the errors I have made.
Not willing to let them go so they can fade.

Stuck in a relationship that is not the best.
A friend who demands and gives me no rest.
Stuck in a place where I don't feel comfortable.
Seeking to find the answer to why I am unable.

Stuck in a pattern of indecisiveness to choose.
A better way to make decisions and lose.
The second-guessing nature that can confuse
Finding a new method to use

DESIGN

I wonder at the design.
God put into creation.
I enjoy the sensation.
God's love shown in nature's sign.

The wonder of our design
I take as a definite sign.
Of the love God has for us
Even when our bodies hurt, and we fuss.

The way each part has a use.
Interdependent, but loose
All our senses provide.
Different cues without divide

God's amazing power
Is shown in our design.
Why do we as humans pine?
Seeking more gifts for God to shower

INNER BEAUTY

Inner beauty shines through and draws you in
A face glows, a peace radiates, and a joy within
Comes out in a smile that reaches the eyes.
And may emit happy cries.

Inner beauty may take your breath away.
Even when faced with loss, it will stay.
There is no price you can put upon it.
It is a gift that will never quit.

Inner beauty can display love.
That God gives from above.
If I had a choice, inner beauty would be.
What I would seek for me